Mastering Python
for Web

Mastering Computer Science
Series Editor: Sufyan bin Uzayr

For more information about this series, please visit: https://www.routledge.com/Mastering-Computer-Science/book-series/MCS

The "Mastering Computer Science" series of books are authored by the Zeba Academy team members, led by Sufyan bin Uzayr.

Zeba Academy is an EdTech venture that develops courses and content for learners primarily in STEM fields, and offers education consulting to Universities and Institutions worldwide. For more info, please visit https://zeba.academy

Mastering Python for Web

A Beginner's Guide

Edited by Sufyan bin Uzayr

CRC Press

Taylor & Francis Group

Boca Raton   London   New York

CRC Press is an imprint of the
Taylor & Francis Group, an **informa** business

First edition published 2022
by CRC Press
6000 Broken Sound Parkway NW, Suite 300, Boca Raton, FL 33487-2742

and by CRC Press
2 Park Square, Milton Park, Abingdon, Oxon, OX14 4RN

CRC Press is an imprint of Taylor & Francis Group, LLC

ISBN: 9781032135670 (hbk)
ISBN: 9781032135656 (pbk)
ISBN: 9781003229896 (ebk)

DOI: 10.1201/9781003229896

Typeset in Minion
by KnowledgeWorks Global Ltd.

Contents

CHAPTER 3 ■ Python Comments and Documentation

About the Editor

Sufyan bin Uzayr is a writer, coder, and entrepreneur with more than a decade of experience in the industry. He has authored several books in the past, pertaining to a diverse range of topics, ranging from History to Computers/IT.

Sufyan is the Director of Parakozm, a multinational IT company specializing in EdTech solutions. He also runs Zeba Academy, an online learning and teaching vertical with a focus on STEM fields.

Sufyan specializes in a wide variety of technologies, such as JavaScript, Dart, WordPress, Drupal, Linux, and Python. He holds multiple degrees, including ones in management, IT, literature, and political science.

Sufyan is a digital nomad, dividing his time between four countries. He has lived and taught in universities and educational institutions around the globe. Sufyan takes a keen interest in technology, politics, literature, history, and sports, and in his spare time, he enjoys teaching coding and English to young students.

Learn more at sufyanism.com.

About the Editor

## CHAPTER 1

Introduction to Python

IN THIS CHAPTER

➢ Introducing Python coding language

➢ Diving into the story of Python creation

➢ Explaining how to install and configure Python

Python is a general-purpose coding language that is used for other types of programming and software development. It is considered a great force in web application creation and systems management and a key driver of the explosion in big data analytics and machine intelligence.

To put simply, Python is generally utilized for things like:

- Writing system scripts
- Processing big data

DOI: 10.1201/9781003229896-1

1

- Performing mathematical computations
- Connecting to database systems
- Reading and modifying files
- Python can be used on Creating web applications on a server
- Creating workflows
- Rapid prototyping
- Production-ready software development
- Back-end web and mobile app development

However, the most typical use case for Python is as a scripting and automation language. When creating scripts, Python is not considered a replacement for shell scripts or batch files but is used to automate interactions with web browsers or application graphical user interfaces (GUI). Thus, with Python, you can create both command-line and cross-platform GUI applications and deploy them as self-contained executables.

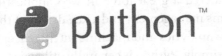

Sophisticated data analysis has become one of the most flourishing areas of IT, and the majority of popular software and data science libraries used for machine learning have

Python interfaces, making it the most popular high-level command interface and numerical algorithms. Python's third-party web frameworks provide fast and convenient ways to create everything from simple lines of code to full-functioning, data-driven sites. Python's latest versions have strong support for operations, enabling sites to handle tens of thousands of requests per second. Python also works as a highly efficient code generator, making it possible to write applications that manipulate their own functions that would be difficult to implement in other languages. This coding is often described as a "glue language," meaning it can make disparate code interoperable again. Thus, if you have applications or program domains that you would like to link with each other, you can use Python for this task.

PYTHON 2 VS. PYTHON 3

Python is available in two different versions: Python 2 and Python 3. Python 2, the older branch, as of January 1, 2020, is no longer supported by its creators, the Python Software Foundation. Python 3, the current and future version of the language, has many updated features that were not included in Python 2, such as new concurrency controls, and a better interpreter. There used to be a lot of competition between the two, but since version 3 incorporated few important functions, it has won over all the Python fan base. Few of those changes in Python 3 included:[1]

- Text vs. Data instead of Unicode vs. 8-bit.

- Print is now a function.

---

[1] https://learntowish.com/history-python-comedy-snake-programming-language/, Learntowish blog

- Views and iterators instead of lists.

- The rules for ordering comparisons have been simplified. So, a heterogeneous list cannot be sorted, because all the elements of a list must be comparable to each other.

At first, Python 3 approval was slowed for some time due to a lack of third-party library support. Because most Python libraries supported only Python 2, it made the transaction to version 3 time consuming. But over the last couple of years, the number of libraries compatible with both Python 2 and Python 3 has increased. Today, Python 3 is the best, up-to-date choice for new projects.

Due to its simplicity, top technology organizations like Dropbox, Google, Mozilla, Hewlett-Packard, IBM, and Cisco have implemented Python for various purposes such as developing, scripting, generation, and software testing. It has also been an inspiration for many other coding languages such as Ruby, Cobra, Boo, CoffeeScript ECMAScript, Groovy, Swift Go, OCaml, and Julia.

The success of Python rests on a strong standard library and a generous assortment of easily obtained and readily used libraries from third-party developers. Python's standard library provides modules for common programming tasks like math, string handling, file and directory access, networking, asynchronous operations, threading, and multi-process management. Additionally, it also includes modules that manage common programming tasks such as reading and writing structured file formats, manipulating compressed files, and working with internet protocols. The default Python distribution also provides a cross-platform

GUI library via Tkinter and an embedded access to the SQLite 3 database.

There are thousands of third-party libraries available through the Python Package Index. For example:

- The BeautifulSoup library provides an all-in-one toolbox for extracting HTML.

- Frameworks like Flask and Django allow rapid development of web services.

- Multiple cloud services can be managed through Python's model using Apache Libcloud.

- Pandas, NumPy and Matplotlib accelerate math and statistical operations, as well as create visualizations of data.

With that said, it is also worth noting the tasks Python is not well suited for. To start with, Python is a high-level language, so it is not the best option for system-level programming—device drivers or OS kernels are inadmissible. It's also not ideal for situations that call for cross-platform standalone binaries. And since everything in the language, including functions and modules themselves, are handled as objects coding comes at the expense of speed. Therefore, it is not the best choice when speed is an absolute priority in every aspect of the application. For that, it is recommended to opt for C/C++ or another language.

Like C#, Java, and Go, Python has garbage-collected memory management, meaning there is no need to implement code to track objects. Garbage collection happens automatically in the background and can pose a performance problem, which is why it is advised to administer it manually or disable it entirely to enhance the performance.

Another compromise comes with Python's use of significant whitespace. As syntactical white space might cause noses to wrinkle, some developers choose not to deal with Python. Another potential turnoff might be the way Python handles variable typing. By default, Python uses dynamic or "duck" typing that can be potentially problematic in large codebases.

With that said, people still appreciate, accept, and simply love using Python. And, there are number of reasons for that:

- **Startups love python:** Startup companies need flexible yet trustworthy programming tool when building their websites, mobile apps, or software programs. The main two priorities then include financial efficiency and capability to stay ahead of schedule. And, because of its ability to be able to deliver on both these objectives, Python is a favored programming language in the startup world.

  Python's efficiency and ease of use result in short development time; and a streamlined QA and debugging process, promise greater return on investment. For someone who wants to become part of the startup community and land a first job and start gaining industry experience, knowing the basics of Python management will make you more attractive as a potential candidate.

- **Python doesn't take long to learn:** For as powerful and multi-functional a language as Python is, it does not take years and few completed degrees to learn Python. Most industry professionals acquired Python basics (that include Python's syntax, keywords, and data types) through a variety of online courses that, on average, take as little as 6–8 weeks. And, shall you have previous experience with coding languages, you might be able to pick it up even faster than that.

- **You can learn python basics for free:** The organization behind Python, the Python Software Foundation hosts a free Python tutorial on their official website: https://www.python.org/about/gettingstarted/. This free resource offers an extensive Python tutorial for beginners, together with material tailored specifically to users with no programming experience, and guidelines for beginners with limited Python programming experience.

  Meanwhile, if you need a more detailed crash course on Python, you can search for it on the web. As mentioned before, there are sites like https://www.learnpython.org/ and https://docs.python-guide.org/ that have additional tutorials. Most of the online platforms make it easy for you to learn the basics of programming and let you get started for free. All you need to do is just sign up.

- **Python has a supportive user community:** Python is an open-source coding language, meaning anyone can modify or create alterations for the Python language. Being open-source also means it is free and allows formations of libraries, frameworks, and extension tools that help to keep the Python language adaptable and compatible over time. It is safe to say that Python's success was realized so far because there is such a supportive community of users engaged with the language.

Moreover, the Python Software Foundation has a dedicated community page on their site linking to several community groups and forums. Users of the Python programming language meet periodically in so-called Python User Groups to share how they use the language and learn new techniques. They also provide great assistance to beginners and offer a platform that allows users to socialize with other people with similar interests. Meetings are usually once every month; they are very informal and open to everyone. And according to the current count, there are about 1,637 Python user groups worldwide in almost 191 cities, 37 countries, and over 860,333 members.[2] You too can find your local Python community through this link: https://wiki.python.org/moin/LocalUserGroups.

The Python Software Foundation is a non-profit organization that offers Grants Program for the implementation of community projects. It processes over 300 requests yearly. Thus, in 2019, the Grants Program provided $324,500 USD in support to initiatives around the world.[3]

---

[2] https://wiki.python.org/moin/LocalUserGroups, wiki Python
[3] https://www.python.org/psf/annual-report/2020/, Python

- **Python is popular:** It matters if a programming language is popular or not. It matters because it would be wrong for you to invest your money and time in learning a language that is not widely used enough and that will not help your job-hunting ambitions.

  According to *The Economist*,[4] Python was the world's most popular coding language in 2018. Other languages like Fortran and Lisp have seen a dramatic decline, and languages like C and C++ remained steady. The article predicted this trend on Python prevalence to stay permanent for quite some time.

- **Python is versatile:** Being general-purpose means that Python language can be used to build parts of different software solutions, which is why major tech corporations like Google and Facebook choose Python programming for their projects. In addition, Python code can also be used to build basic programs, and as a developer, you can have an incredibly wide range of work options. Whether you want to go work for a tech giant, build your own software programs, or work as a freelance web developer, knowledge of Python programming is considered to be a strength that can make any of these plans possible.

- **Python ensures that the front and back ends of your projects work better together:** If you want to have a great career as a developer, it would be useful to know that your goal might be to sync and balance

---

[4] https://www.economist.com/graphic-detail/2018/07/26/python-is-becoming-the-worlds-most-popular-coding-language, *The Economist*

the front end and back end made up of databases and web servers that power the front end of the website applications.

And when we named Python a "glue language," we meant that it is used to script back-end actions, allowing your digital product's front and back ends to work in harmony. So, if you are looking to add server-side or back-end skills to your front-end developer set of competencies, learning Python might be a perfect way to start with.

- **Python is customizable:** If you need a customizable programming language, then Python must be a perfect option. Just like JavaScript, there is no shortage of libraries and frameworks for Python to shape and deliver your specific coding needs.

  Popular Python fully featured server-side web framework like Django is created to make Python more practical at tuning web applications, while PyQt is a framework that allows Python to build GUIs user interfaces that include the use of on-screen icons and graphics to operate user commands.

- **Python is a great tool for processes automation:** One of the essential but tedious parts of working in tech is administering all the repetitive, time-consuming, tech-related processes. Boring tasks like copying files, dragging folders and renaming files, managing assets to servers—all of these accumulatively take a lot of precious time. In this case, automation via Python implementation could be your savior. Python's ability to write system scripts enables you to create simple Python programs to automate routine tasks that take so much of your productivity. The time you will be able to save by readjusting your processes with Python is a hugely appealing aspect of learning the language.

- **Python gives you the tools to work anywhere in tech:** Learning Python code will not only secure your potential expertise in internet development—it will prepare you for a variety of future tech jobs. Python is used for more than traditional web development. As a matter of fact, Python is a top language for such popular emerging scientific fields, including data analysis, artificial intelligence, machine learning, and data science. Therefore, knowing the language will help to keep your options open, and you may have more tech-related opportunities if you decide to master Python.

A BRIEF HISTORY OF PYTHON

Python is a general-purpose, high-level programming language that was initially designed by Guido van Rossum in 1991 and developed by Python Software Foundation. It was mainly developed for advancing code readability, and its syntax that would allow programmers to express concepts in shorter code.

Official work on Python started in the late 1980s. Soon after that, Guido van Rossum began doing its application-based trial in December 1989 at Centrum Wiskunde & Informatica (CWI) in the Netherland. Originally, the Python project has started as a hobby because he was looking for interesting work to keep him occupied during

Christmas. Python's programming language is based on ABC Programming Language, which had the interfacing with the microkernel-based Amoeba Operating System that turned a collection of single-board computers into a transparent distributed system. Van Rossum had already helped create ABC earlier in his career and had seen some issues. So, he took the syntax of ABC, some of its best features, and fixed other unsettled attributes. And just like that, by correcting those issues completely, he had created a new scripting language.

The language was released in 1991. When it was released, it used many codes and had a distinguished design approach. Its main objective was to provide code readability and advance developers' overall productivity.

But what about the name "Python"? Most people think that since the logo depicts two snakes, the origin of the name must have been inspired by the actual python snake. Surprisingly, that is far from the truth. Guido van Rossum, the creator of Python, wrote in 1996 about the origin of the name of his programming language that lays in British humor rather than anything else: "Over six years ago, in December 1989, I was looking for a 'hobby' programming project that would keep me occupied during the week around Christmas. My office … would be closed, but I had a home computer and not much else on my hands. I decided to write an interpreter for the new scripting language I had been thinking about lately: a descendant of ABC that would appeal to Unix/C hackers. I chose Python as a working title for the project, being in a slightly irreverent mood and a big fan of Monty Python's Flying Circus."[5]

Moreover, in 2004 the Python community came up with guiding principles for Python design and called it "The Zen of Python":[6]

> Beautiful is better than ugly.
> Explicit is better than implicit.
> Simple is better than complex.
> Complex is better than complicated.
> Flat is better than nested.
> Sparse is better than dense.
> Readability counts.
> Special cases aren't special enough to break the
>   rules.
> Although practicality beats purity.
> Errors should never pass silently.
> Unless explicitly silenced.
> In the face of ambiguity, refuse the temptation
>   to guess.

---

[5] https://www.python.org/doc/essays/foreword/, Python
[6] https://www.python.org/dev/peps/pep-0020/, Python

> There should be one—and preferably only one—
> obvious way to do it.
> Although that way may not be obvious at first
> unless you're Dutch.
> Now is better than never.
> Although never is often better than *right* now.
> If the implementation is hard to explain, it's a
> bad idea.
> If the implementation is easy to explain, it may
> be a good idea.
> Namespaces are one honking great idea—let's
> do more of those!

For many years after launching, Python did not do well. Trusted solutions like ASP.NET, Java, and PHP dominated the enterprise. Python seriously took off only in the 2000s when new startups started using Python for their projects. Many low-budget businesses also prioritized Python because of its ease of use, rapid development, and certainly due to the low cost to host it.

Python has hit the top of its popularity when Dropbox was introduced in the market. One day, the story states that an MIT student named Drew Houston forgot his USB flash drive for his class one day. He later started thinking about a better solution for sharing files. Houston started a company named Evenflow back in 2007 with a single product named Dropbox. For the first time, Dropbox software enabled people to create a folder on their computer that's automatically uploaded to service in the cloud, and it's automatically synced to all the devices that the user has installed Dropbox on. The company reached a million users by April 2009. By the end of 2009, they had 3 million users. Dropbox was written in Python.

Dropbox soon became a showcase of successful Python implementation. An interesting point is that Dropbox was originally written in Python 2. And in 2013, when Guido van Rossum joined Dropbox, he was mainly responsible for converting the software to newly Python 3. He worked for Dropbox until his retirement. After seeing Python scale so well with Dropbox, many other enterprises started considering it for their business.

The late 2000s was also the time when social media exploded. And as its influence was growing, so did the amount of data that it had to manage. At the same time, Python quickly became the language of choice for accessing that data, especially in the tech, startup world. During the financial crisis of 2008, automation took over the financial world. Financial institutions had the need to process big data and started looking at data to spot patterns, make decisions, and manage economic processes. Corporations had plenty of data but no simple and clear way to access it. That is when they commenced performing quantitative analysis on financial data using Python. Other packages such as NumPy, scikit, and Matplotlib had a comparatively heavy development background, and Python soon became the top choice for data science.

There was another driver for Python that made it the go-to language for data science, the boot camps. And as web development exploded, so did boot camps. Python has always been free to access, learning the language. And, consequently, the first language taught in many of these boot camp programs was Python. High schools and colleges all around the world started teaching coding as a core skill, and much of that was based on Python.

Nowadays, if you want to become a full-stack developer, you usually need to start with the basis of front-end and back-end software. Many instructional programs have established the transition from JavaScript to Python to be smooth for first-time learners, even though the languages are different. So, if one day you end up as a front-end developer working on JavaScript and interacting with an application programming interface (API), you might find creating a back end for these applications pretty tedious, until you try Python. Its frameworks such as Flask and Django offer easy solutions for developers who want to build more back-end software and create powerful APIs to coordinate properly.

INSTALLING AND CONFIGURING PYTHON

Any crash course on Python is likely to start with installing or updating Python on your computer. There are multiple methods of installation: you can download official Python distributions from Python.org, install from a package manager, and even install specialized distributions for scientific computing.

If you are learning how to navigate Python on your own, the best option would be to start at Python.org. This platform represents the official distribution, and that kind of source is generally the safest option for learning to program in Python.

On the platform, you can easily get access to a variety of useful tutorials and all sorts of learning materials:

- How to check which version of Python is installed on our device.

- How to install and update Python on Windows, macOS, and Linux.

- How to use Python on mobile devices like phones or tablets.

- How to use Python on the web with online interpreters.

And before we go on covering each one of these points, it is important to get acquainted with few of top-level directories in the CPython source tree that are meant to help you find where a certain piece of functionality is implemented.[7]

- **Doc:** the official documentation. This is what https://docs.python.org/ uses.

- **Grammar:** contains the EBNF grammar file for Python.

---

[7] https://devguide.python.org/setup/, Python

- **Include:** contains all interpreter-wide header files.

- **Lib:** the part of the standard library implemented in pure Python.

- **Mac:** Mac-specific code (e.g., using IDLE as an OS X application).

- **Misc:** things that do not belong elsewhere. Typically, this is varying kinds of developer-specific documentation.

- **Modules:** the part of the standard library (plus some other code) that is implemented in C.

- **Objects:** code for all built-in types.

- **PC:** Windows-specific code.

- **PC build:** build files for the version of MSVC currently used for the Windows installers provided on python.org.

- **Parser:** code related to the parser. The definition of the AST nodes is also kept here.

- **Programs:** source code for C executables, including the main function for the CPython interpreter (in versions prior to Python 3.5, these files are in the Modules directory).

- **Python:** the code that makes up the core CPython runtime. This includes the compiler, eval loop, and various built-in modules.

- **Tools:** various tools that are (or have been) used to maintain Python.

HOW TO INSTALL PYTHON ON WINDOWS

Unlike many other Unix systems and services, Windows does not include a system-supported installation of Python. In order to make Python available, the CPython team has advanced Windows installers with every version for many years now. These installers are primarily created to add a per-user installation of Python, including the core interpreter and library.

As of now, there are three installation methods on Windows:

1. The Microsoft Store

2. The Full Installer

3. Windows Subsystem for Linux

If you want to check whether you already have Python on your Windows or not, you need to first open a command-line application, such as PowerShell. You can do it by following these three simple steps:

1. Press the Win key

2. Type PowerShell

3. Press Enter

As an alternative, you can press the right-click on the *Start* button and select *Windows PowerShell* or *Windows PowerShell (Admin)*. One can also use cmd.exe or Windows Terminal (a multi-tabbed command-line that Microsoft has developed for Windows 10, which later completely replaced the Windows Console). With the command line open, type in the following command and press Enter :

```
C:\> python -version
Python 3.9.2.
Using the --version switch will show you
the version that's installed.
Alternatively, you can use the -V switch:
C:\> python -V
Python 3.9.2.
```

In either case, if you see a version less than 3.9.2., which was the most recent version at the time of writing, then you might want to upgrade your installation. And if you do not have a version of Python on your system, then both of the above commands are programmed to launch the Microsoft Store and redirect you to the Python application page.

And if you do not know where exactly the installation is located, you can find it out through the where.exe command in cmd.exe or PowerShell:

```
C:\> where.exe python
C:\Users\mertz\AppData\Local\Programs\
Python\Python37-32\python.exe
 (Note that the where.exe command will
work only if Python has been installed.)
```

As mentioned before, there are three hassle-free ways to install the official Python distribution on Windows:

1. **Microsoft Store package:** The simplest installation method on Windows through the Microsoft Store app. This method is mostly advised for beginner

Python users looking for an easy setup multimedia experience.

2. **Full Installer:** This option involves downloading Python directly from the Python.org official website. This is recommended for intermediate and advanced developers who need more functionality and control during the installation process.

3. **Windows Subsystem for Linux (WSL):** The WSL can let you run a Linux environment directly in Windows. You can learn how to enable and manage the WSL by reading the Windows Subsystem for Linux Installation Guide for Windows 10.

You can also complete the installation on Windows using alternative platforms, such as Anaconda (https://www.anaconda.com/), which is a great interactive website for doing scientific computing and data science with Python. By accessing the website, you can learn how to install Anaconda on Windows, through Setting Up Python for Machine Learning on Windows.

In this chapter, we are only going to focus on only the first two installation options, since they are the most convenient and therefore popular installation methods in a Windows community.

The two official Python installers for Windows are quite different. The Microsoft Store package has specific limitations. The official Python documentation states the following in regards to the Microsoft Store package—precisely that it is "intended mainly for interactive use." Meaning that the Microsoft Store package is designed to be used by students and people learning to use Python for the first time. And since this method is mostly targeting Python beginners, the Microsoft Store package is considered to be ill-suited for a professional development environment. Moreover, it does not have full write access to shared locations such as TEMP or the registry, which could be major deal-breakers for expert developers.

But if you are new to Python and for the time being only focused on learning the basics of language rather than building professional software, then you should go ahead and install it from the Microsoft Store package. It will offer the shortest and easiest way to getting started with minimal fuss. On the other hand, if you are one of the more experienced developers looking to develop professional software in a Windows environment, then the official Python.org installer would be an answer for you. In that case, your installation and configuration will not be restricted by Microsoft Store policies, and you can control the execution process and add Python to PATH if necessary.

How to Install from the Microsoft Store

As mentioned, if you are an absolute newbie to Python and looking to get started quickly, then the Microsoft Store package is the best option to get you accustomed to Python potential. Simply put, you can install it from the Microsoft Store in just one step.

Step 1: Open the Python App Page in the Microsoft Store. Open the Microsoft Store application start to search for Python. Here, you are likely to see multiple versions that you can choose to install. Make sure you select Python 3.9.2, or the highest version number you can find available in the application store, to open the installation page. Another thing to keep in mind is that you have to pay attention to who the application was produced by. The official Python application that you want to be installed should be the one created by the Python Software Foundation. The official Microsoft Store package will always be free, so if the application costs money, then it is not the original one. Alternatively, you can open PowerShell and type the following command:

```
C:\> python
```

If you do not have a version of Python on your system yet, then if you press Enter, the Microsoft Store will automatically launch you to the latest version of Python in the store. And once you have selected the version to be installed, follow *these simple steps to complete the installation*:

1. Click *Get*.

2. Wait for the application to start downloading. When it's finished downloading, instead of the *Get* button you will see a different button that says *Install on my devices*.

3. Click *Install on my devices* and select the devices on which you would like to complete the installation.

4. Click *Install Now* and then *OK* to start the installation.

5. Once the installation is successfully completed, you will see the following message at the top of the Microsoft Store page: "This product is installed."

How to Install from the Full Installer

For professional developers, who look for a full-featured Python development options, installing from the full installer is the correct choice. It enables more customization and lets you take control over the installation, unlike if you choose to install from the Microsoft Store. You can install from the full installer in two steps.

Step 1: You have to download the Full Installer following these steps:

1. Open a browser window and navigate to the Python. org Downloads page for Windows.

2. Under the "Python Releases for Windows" button, click the link for the Latest Python 3 Release. And as of now, the latest version was Python 3.9.2.

3. Scroll to the bottom and select either *Windows x86-64 executable installer for 64-bit* or *Windows x86 executable installer for 32-bit*.

    If you are not sure whether to select the 32-bit or the 64-bit installer, then you can expand the box below to help you decide.

Step 2: Run the Installer

Once you have completed downloading an installer, run it by double-clicking on the downloaded file. A dialog box like the one below will appear. There would be four things you need to notice about this dialog box:

1. The default install path is in the AppData/directory of the current Windows user.

2. The *Customize installation* button is usually used to customize the installation location and which additional features get installed, including pip and IDLE.

3. The *Install launcher for all users* checkbox is checked default. This means every user on the machine will have access to the py.exe launcher. You can uncheck this box to restrict Python to the current Windows user.

4. The *Add Python 3.9 to PATH* checkbox is unchecked by default. There might be several drawbacks that might change your mind to not wanting Python on PATH, so make sure you understand the implications before you check this box.

The full installer hands you total control over the installation process. You can customize the installation to meet your needs using the options available in the dialog box. All you need to do after that is just to click *Install Now*.

HOW TO INSTALL PYTHON ON macOS

Python 2 as well as other programming languages like Ruby, and Perl used to come preinstalled on older versions of macOS. However, it is no longer the case for current versions of macOS, starting with macOS Catalina. Naturally, there are two claimed installation methods on macOS:

1. The official installer

2. The Homebrew package manager

To start with, you might need to check which Python version you have on your Mac. You can do it by opening a command-line application, such as Terminal. And, here is how you open Terminal:

1. Press the Cmd + Space keys

2. Type Terminal

3. Press Enter

Alternatively, you can go through opening Finder and navigating to *Applications → Utilities → Terminal*. With the command line open, try typing in the following commands:

1. # Check the system Python version
   $ python –version

2. # Check the Python 2 version
   $ python2 –version

3. # Check the Python 3 version
   $ python3 –version

And if you have Python on your system, then one or more of these commands would automatically respond with a version number. You might want to get the latest version of Python if any of these conditions is true:

- None of the above commands come up with a version number.

- The only version you see displayed is in the Python 2.X series.

- You have a version of Python 3 that is not the newest available.

As mentioned earlier, there are two ways to install the official Python distribution on macOS:

1. **The official installer:** This method requires downloading the official installer from the Python.org website.

2. **The Homebrew package manager:** This method involves first downloading and installing the Homebrew package manager if you do not have it installed yet, and then typing a command into a terminal application.

Both the official installer and the Homebrew package manager are great to work with, but the Python Software Foundation supports only the official installer. And since the distributions installed by the official installer and the Homebrew package manager are not similar, installing from Homebrew comes with a few limitations.

The Python distribution for macOS on Homebrew does not include the Tcl/Tk dependency required by the standard Python interface, Tkinter module. Tkinter is the customary library module for developing GUI in Python and also an interface for the Tk GUI toolkit. And since Homebrew does not install the Tk GUI toolkit dependency, it still relies on an existing version installed on your system. The system version of Tcl/Tk may be outdated and could eventually prevent you from importing the Tkinter module.

The Homebrew package manager is a popular method because Homebrew is a command-line utility, and can be automated with basic scripts. Additionally, installing Python on macOS is preferable by many since it is easy to manage from the command line and easy to upgrade without having to go to a website. At the same time, the Python distribution offered by Homebrew is not supported by the Python Software Foundation and therefore not fully reliable. The most secure method on macOS is still to use the official installer, especially if you would need Python GUI programming with Tkinter.

How to Install from the Official Installer

As stated before, installing Python from the official installer is the most reliable installation method on macOS. It offers all the system dependencies needed for developing applications with Python. You can install from the official installer in two simple steps.

Step 1: Download the Official Installer by following these steps:

1. Open a browser window and navigate to the Python. org Downloads page for macOS.

2. Under the "Python Releases for Mac OS X" heading, click on the *Latest Python 3 Release*. As of now, the latest version is Python 3.9.2.

3. Scroll to the bottom and click *macOS 64-bit installer* to start the download.

Step 2: Run the Installer by double-clicking the down-loaded file. You should be able to see the following window:

1. Press *Continue* until you are asked to agree to the software license agreement. Then click *Agree*.

2. You will then see a window that tells you the install destination and asks how much space you want it to take. You most likely do not need to change the default location, so go continue by clicking *Install* to start the installation.

3. When the installer is finished copying files, click *Close* to close the installer window.

How to Install from Homebrew

For users who need to install from the command line, and do not need to develop GUI with the Tkinter module, the Homebrew package manager would be a perfect option. You can install it from the Homebrew package manager in two steps.

Step 1: Install Homebrew (in case you already have Homebrew installed, then you can skip this step) following this procedure:

1. Open a browser and go to http://brew.sh/

2. You should see a command for installing Homebrew near the top of the page under the title "Install Homebrew."

3. Highlight this command with your cursor and press Cmd + C to copy it to your clipboard.

4. Open a terminal window and paste the command, then press Enter. This way you have started the Homebrew installation.

5. Enter your macOS user password when requested.
   It may take a few minutes to download all of Homebrew's required files, but it is done, you will end up back at the shell prompt in your terminal window. If you are doing this on macOS for the first time, you may get a pop-up alert asking you to install Apple's command line developer tools. These tools are a prerequisite for installation, so you need to confirm the dialog box by clicking Install. And after the developer tools are installed, you should press Enter to continue the installation of Homebrew. And once Homebrew is installed, you are ready to install Python.

Step 2: Install Python by following these steps:

1. Open a terminal application.

2. Type in the following command to upgrade Homebrew: $brew update && brew upgrade
   This will download and set up the latest version of Python on your computer. You can make sure everything went correctly by testing it through the Terminal:

   1. Open a terminal.

   2. Type pip3 and press Enter.

3. You should see the text from Python's pip package manager. If you get an error message running pip3, you should go through the install steps again to make sure you have not missed any steps.

HOW TO INSTALL PYTHON ON LINUX

In this section, you are going to learn about Python installation methods on Linux and as a result, will hopefully be able to complete it yourself. Usually, many Linux distributions already come packaged with Python, but it probably will not be the latest version or could even be Python 2 instead of Python 3. You will need to check the version yourself just to make sure. In order to find out which version of Python you have, proceed to open a terminal window and try the following commands:

```
# Check the system Python version
$ python -version

# Check the Python 2 version
$ python2 -version

# Check the Python 3 version
$ python3 -version
```

If you already have Python on your computer, then one or more of these commands should come up with a version number. Typically, there are two convenient and comparatively fast ways to install the official Python distribution on Linux:

1. **Install from a package manager:** This is the most popular installation method on most Linux distributions. It requires running a command from the command line.

2. **Build from source code:** This method is more complex than using a package manager. It involves running a series of commands from the command line and at the same time making sure you have the correct dependencies installed to complete the Python source code.

Unfortunately, not every Linux distribution has a package manager, and not every package manager has Python in its set. Judging by your operating system, building Python from source code could be your only option. Which installation method you are going to use mainly depends on whether your Linux OS has a package manager and whether you want to control the details of the installation.

The most popular to this day way to install Python on Linux is with your operating system's package manager. It is considered to be a default choice by many expert developers. However, depending on your Linux distribution, Python may not be available through a package manager. In this case, you will have to build up Python from source code.

There are three main reasons that could limit you into choosing to build Python from source code:

1. You will not be able to download Python from your operating system's package manager.

2. If you might need to lower the memory footprint on embedded systems, you will want to control how Python gets compiled.

3. You want to be able to test beta versions and release candidates of the latest and most advanced version before it becomes available.

In order to complete the installation on your Linux machine, find your Linux distribution below and follow the steps provided.

How to Install on Ubuntu and Linux Mint

Depending on which version of the Ubuntu distribution you have, the process for setting up Python on your system will vary accordingly. You can determine your local Ubuntu version by typing the following command:

```
$ lsb_release -a
No LSB modules are available.
Distributor ID: Ubuntu
Description: Ubuntu 16.04.4 LTS
Release: 16.04
Codename: xenial
```

Follow the guideline below that match the version number you get under Release heading in the console output:

- **Ubuntu 18.04, Ubuntu 20.04 and above:** Python 3.9 does not come by default on Ubuntu 18.04 and above, but it is available in the Universe repository. To install version 3.9, you will need to open a terminal application and type the following commands:

    - $ sudo apt-get update

    - $ sudo apt-get install python3.9 python3-pip

And when the installation is complete, you can now run Python 3.9 with the python3.9 command and pip with the pip3 command.

- **Linux Mint and Ubuntu 17 and below:** Python 3.9 is not in the Universe repository, so you would have to get it from a Personal Package Archive (PPA). For instant, to install from the "deadsnakes" PPA, use the following commands:

  - $ sudo add-apt-repository PPA:dead snakes/PPA

  - $ sudo apt-get update

  - $ sudo apt-get install python3.9 python3-pip

How to Install on Debian Linux

Before you can install Python 3.9 on Debian, you will have to install the sudo command. In order to do that, you should execute the following commands in a terminal:

```
$ su
$ apt-get install sudo
$ sudo vim /etc/sudoers
```

Right after that, try opening the/etc/sudoers file using the sudo vim command or your favorite text editor. Add the following line of text to the end of the file, replacing your_ username with your actual username: your_username ALL=(ALL) ALL

Completing that, you can go ahead and skip until you reach How to Build Python From Source Code section to finish installing Python.

How to Install on openSUSE

Building from the source is the most reliable way to set up Python on openSUSE. To do that, you will need to install the development tools, which can be done in YaST operating system setup via the menus or by using Zipper, the command line package manager:

```
$ sudu zypper install -t pattern devel_C_C
```

As it will have to install more than 150 packages, it is considered a normal practice that might take a while to complete. But once it is done, feel free to skip ahead to the How to Build Python From Source Code section.

How to Install on CentOS and Fedora

Unfortunately, Python 3.9 is not available in the CentOS and Fedora repositories, so you are expected to build Python from source code. Before you install Python, though, you need to make sure your system is prepared beforehand. At first, update the yum package manager through the following code: $ sudo yum -y update

And once yum finishes updating, you can freely install the necessary build dependencies with the following line of commands:

```
$ sudo yum -y groupinstall "Development
Tools"
$ sudo yum -y install GCC OpenSSL-devel
bzip2-devel libffi-devel
```

And when you see that everything is finished installing, you can skip ahead to the How to Build Python From Source Code section.

How to Install on Arch Linux

Arch Linux is popular for adhering to the KISS principle ("Keep It Simple, Stupid") and mostly focused on modernity and pragmatism. That said, Arch Linux is fairly diligent about keeping up with Python releases. It is very much likely you already have the latest version installed by default. If not, you can use the following command to update Python: $ packman -S python. And once it is finished updating, you are all set to start scripting.

HOW TO BUILD PYTHON FROM SOURCE CODE

In cases when your Linux distribution does not have the latest version of Python, or when you just want to be able to build the latest, fastest version yourself, you can take the following steps to be able to build Python from source:

Step 1: Download the source code

To start, you need to get the Python source code through the Python.org. All you have to do is go to the Downloads page and look for the latest source for Python 3 at the top. Make sure you are searching for Python 3 and not Python 2.

When you select the Python 3 version, you can see a "Files" section at the bottom of the page. Select *Gzipped source tarball* and download it to your machine. If you prefer a command-line method, you can use Wget program that retrieves content from web servers to download the file to your current directory:

```
$ wget https://www.python.org/ftp/
python/3.8.4/Python-3.8.4.tgz
```

When the tarball completes downloading, you will then need to take care of other things to prepare your system for building Python.

Step 2: Prepare your system

There are a few fixed steps involved in building Python from scratch. The aim of each one of those steps is the same on all distros, but you might need to translate it to your distribution if it does not use apt-get:

1. First, make sure you have updated your package manager and upgraded your packages:

```
$ sudo apt-get update
$ sudo apt-get upgrade
```

2. Next, you need to have all of the build requirements installed:

```
# For apt-based systems (like Debian,
Ubuntu, and Mint)
$ sudo apt-get install -y make build-
essential libssl-dev zlib1g-dev\

libbz2-dev libreadline-dev libsqlite3-
dev wget curl llvm\
libncurses5-dev libncursesw5-dev
xz-utils tk-dev
# For yum-based systems (like CentOS)
$ sudo yum -y groupinstall "Development
Tools"
$ sudo yum -y install gcc openssl-
devel bzip2-devel libffi-devel
```

And if you already have some of the requirements installed on your system, it is not going to create any problem because you can execute the above commands and any existing packages will not be overwritten.

Step 3: Build Python

1. Once you have all the prerequisites and the Tape Archive (TAR) files, you can start unpacking the source into a directory. Please note that the following command will create a new directory called Python-3.9.1 under the one you're in:

```
$ tar xvf Python-3.9.2.tgz
$ cd Python-3.9.2.
```

2. Now, you need to run the ./configure tool to prepare the build:

```
$./configure-enable-optimizations-with-
ensurepip=install
```

The enable-optimizations flag will enable some optimizations within Python to make it run about 10 percent faster. Doing this may add twenty or thirty minutes to the compilation time.

3. Next, you build Python using the -j option that simply tells make to split the building into parallel steps to speed up the compilation. Even with the parallel builds, this step can take several minutes:

```
$ make -j 8
```

4. Finally, you will want to install your new version of Python. You can use the altinstall option here to avoid overwriting the system Python. Since you are installing into/usr/bin, you will need to run as root:

```
$ sudo make altinstall
```

The overall installation might take some time, but once it is done, you are advised to verify that Python is set up correctly.

Step 4: Verify your installation

You can test that the python3.9 –version command returns the latest version:

```
$ python3.9 -version
Python 3.9.2.
And if you see Python 3.9.2., then
your installation is fully verified
```

In case you want to run extra testing, you might also choose the test suite to make sure everything is working properly and swiftly on your system. To run the test suite, you just have to type the following command:

```
$ python3.8 -m test
```

You do not need to rush this part because your computer will be running tests for some time. And if all the tests pass without an error, then you can be confident that your brand-new Python build is working as expected.

HOW TO INSTALL PYTHON ON iOS

The Pythonista software application for iOS is a fully developed Python creative environment that you can run on your iPhone or iPad. It has all the features including a Python editor, technical documentation, and an interpreter, all integrated into a single app.

Pythonista could be a great tool for someone who does not like to be stuck with just the laptop and prefers working or polishing their Python skills on the go. The application comes with the complete Python 3 standard library and also includes full documentation that you can browse offline. To set up Pythonista, all you need to do is download it from the iOS app store.

HOW TO INSTALL PYTHON ON ANDROID

And if you are not Apple but an Android fan, and want to practice Python from your tablet or phone, it has been taken care of as well. Android app that reliably supports Python 3.8 is Pydroid 3. Hydroid 3 features an interpreter that you can use for read–eval–print loop (REPL), interactive language sessions, and it also allows you to edit, save, and execute Python code. Additionally, it has built-in C, C++, and even Fortran compiler specially for Pydroid 3. With it, you can build any library from pip, as wells as build and install dependencies from a command line.

You can download and install Pydroid 3 free version and paid Premium version (supports code prediction and code analysis) from the Google Play Store.

ONLINE PYTHON INTERPRETERS

If you are looking for examples and live Python tutorials without actually having to set it up on your machine, then there are several websites that can offer that online Python interpretation. These cloud-based Python interpreters may not be able to execute some of the more complex activities, but they are quite adequate for running most of the code and maybe a nice way to get started if you are a beginner.

- **Python.org Online Console:** https://www.python.org/shell/

- **Repl.it:** https://replit.com/

- **Trinket:** https://trinket.io/
- **Python Anywhere:** https://www.pythonanywhere.com/

REGENERATE CONFIGURE

If a change is made to Python which relies on some Portable Operating System Interface (POSIX) system-specific functionality, it is important to update the configure script to test for its functionality.

Python's configure script is generated from configure.ac using Autoconf tool for producing scripts for building and packaging software on computer systems. Instead of editing configure, make sure you edit configure.ac and then run autoreconf to regenerate configure and a number of other files.

Just like with any other software, under some rare instances, you may encounter Python errors in scripts like Parser/asdl_c.py or Python/makeopcodetargets.py. Since Python auto-generates some of its own code, you need a full build from scratch to run the auto-generation scripts. To overcome this problem, auto-generated files are also checked into the virtual storage, Git repository.

Python is used widely enough that practically all code editors have used some form of support when writing Python code for the first time. And if you are looking for some additional tools or special guidelines to administer coding in Python, you can search for those in Additional Resources and Developer's Guide: https://devguide. python.org/#resources. There you can find exceptional materials on exploring CPython's internals, changing

CPython's grammar, design of CPython's compiler, design of CPython's garbage collector as well as basic Tool support option. Python.org maintenance also includes dynamic analysis with clang and various tools with configuration files as found in the Misc directory.

## CHAPTER 2

Python Data Type

IN THIS CHAPTER

➤ Introducing main Python data types

➤ Talking about each type's in-built method descriptions

➤ Explaining how to access, update and modify Python data types

Data analysis is a very important field at the moment. Most companies would like to have a professional data analyst on board to take care of a massive database and prevent any unexpected errors from happening. A good data analyst is one who knows how to use various programming tools to manage large amounts of complex data and find relevant information from it. In short, if you are the one looking for a place in the ever-evolving IT area, potentially as a data analyst, you need to start investing in skills in the following areas, in order to be valued in the workplace:

- **Domain Expertise:** You need to have domain expertise to be able to process big data and come up with insights that are relevant to their workplace.

- **Programming Skills:** Data analysts should possess programming skills to know the right libraries to use in order to clean data, mine, and gain insights from it.

- **Statistics:** An analyst will not be able to derive full meaning from data without knowing how to use some basic statistical tools.

- **Visualization Skills:** A data analyst cannot present raw data as a result of their work, he would need to have great data visualization skills, in order to summarize and present comprehensive data to a third party.

- **Storytelling:** At last, an analyst needs to communicate their findings to a stakeholder or client. This means that they will not only have to create a data story but also have the ability to narrate it.

A data type is basically just an internal construct that a programming language uses to store and manipulate the rest of the data. Despite how well Python works, at some point in data analysis processes, everyone will likely need to explicitly convert data from one type to another. In this chapter, we will discuss the basic Python data types, how they map, and what are the options for converting from one data type to another. Simply said, data types are the classification or categorization of data items. Python supports the following built-in data types:

- **Scalar types**

  - **Int:** Integers stand for positive or negative whole numbers (without a fractional part). Bitwise operations that are used in bit-level programming, only make sense for integers. The priorities of the binary bitwise operations are all lower than the numeric operations and higher than the comparisons. And the unary operation ~ has the same priority as the other unary numeric operations (+ and -).[1]

This table lists the bitwise operations sorted in ascending priority:

x | y	bitwise or of x and y
x ^ y	bitwise exclusive or of x and y
x & y	bitwise and of x and y
x ≪ n	x shifted left by n bits
x ≫ n	x shifted right by n bits
~x	the bits of x inverted

---

[1] https://docs.python.org/3/library/stdtypes.html, Python

Additional Methods on Integer Types

The int type implements the numbers and integral abstract base class. In addition, it provides a few more operational methods:[2]

1. **int.bit_length():** Return the number of bits necessary to represent an integer in binary, excluding the sign and leading zeros.

2. **int.to_bytes(length, byteorder, *, signed=False):** Return an array of bytes representing an integer.

3. **classmethod int.from_bytes(bytes, byteorder, *, signed=False):** Return the integer represented by the given array of bytes.

4. **int.as_integer_ratio():** Return a pair of integers whose ratio is exactly equal to the original integer and with a positive denominator. The integer ratio of integers (whole numbers) is always the integer as the numerator and 1 as the denominator.

   i. **Float:** Represents real number with a floating-point representation in which a fractional component is denoted by a decimal symbol or scientific notation. The float type implements the numbers and real abstract base class. It also has the following additional methods:[3]

   1. **float.as_integer_ratio():** Return a pair of integers whose ratio is exactly equal to the original float and with a positive denominator.

---

[2] https://docs.python.org/3/library/stdtypes.html, Python

[3] https://docs.python.org/3/library/stdtypes.html, Python

2. **float.is_integer()**: Return True if the float instance is finite with integral value, and False otherwise:

```
>>>
>>> (-2.0).is_integer()
True
>>> (3.2).is_integer()
False
```

Two methods support conversion to and from hexadecimal strings. Since Python's floats are stored internally as binary numbers, converting a float to or from a decimal string usually involves a small rounding error. In contrast, hexadecimal strings allow exact representation and specification of floating-point numbers. This can be useful when debugging and in numerical work.

3. **float.hex()**: Return a representation of a floating-point number as a hexadecimal string. For finite floating-point numbers, this representation will always include a leading 0x and a trailing p and exponent.

4. **classmethod float.fromhex(s)**: Class method to return the float represented by a hexadecimal string s. The string s may have leading and trailing whitespace. Note that float.hex() is an instance method, while float.fromhex() is a class method.

   i. **Complex:** A number that consists of a real and imaginary component represented as x + 2y.

   ii. **Bool:** Data that has one of two built-in values True or False. Notice that "T" and "F" are capital.

iii. **None:** The None represents the null object in Python or by functions that do not explicitly return a value.

- **Sequence type:** A sequence means an ordered collection of similar or different data types. Python has the following built-in sequence data types:

  - **String:** a string value simply represents a collection of one or more characters put in single, double, or triple quotes.
  - **List:** a list here stands for an ordered collection of one or more data items, not necessarily of the same type, but in square brackets.
  - **Tuple:** a Tuple object is an ordered collection of one or more data items, not necessarily of the same type, put in parentheses.

- **Mapping type**

  - **Dictionary:** A dictionary Dict() object is a collection of data in a key:value pair form. Such pairs have to be enclosed in curly brackets. For example: {1:"Sam," 2:"Ben, 3:"Roy, 4:"Molly"}

- **Set types**

  - **set:** The set in Python is the same as the implementation of the set in Mathematics. A set object has suitable methods to perform mathematical set operations like union, intersection, difference, etc. In scripting, it goes as a mutable, unordered collection of distinct hashable objects.
  - **frozenset:** frozen, unlike the ordinary set, is an immutable version of sets whose elements are added from other data types.

- **Mutable and immutable types:** Mutable data objects of the above-mentioned data types are stored in a computer's memory for processing. Some of these values can be modified during processing, but once they are created in the memory, their content cannot be altered. Numbers, strings, and Tuples are immutable, which means their contents cannot be changed after creation.

- **Iterator types:** Python supports a concept of iteration over containers and is using container user-defined classes to support iteration. Sequences, described below in more detail, always support the iteration methods:

1. **container.__iter__():** Return an iterator object. This process is required to support the iterator protocol described below, and if a container supports different types of iteration, additional methods can be provided to specifically request iterators for those iteration types. This method corresponds to the tp_ iter slot of the type structure for Python objects in the Python/C application programming interface (API).

   The iterator objects themselves are required to support the following two methods, which together form the iterator protocol:[4]

2. **iterator.__iter__():** Return the iterator object itself. This is required to allow both containers and iterators to be used with the for and in statements. This method

---

[4] https://docs.python.org/3/library/stdtypes.html, Python

corresponds to the tp_iter slot of the type structure for Python objects in the Python/C API.

3. **iterator.__next__()**: Return the next item from the container. If there are no further items, raise the StopIteration exception. This method corresponds to the tp_iternext slot of the type structure for Python objects in the Python/C API. Once an iterator's __next__() method raises StopIteration, it must continue to do so on subsequent calls. Implementations that do not obey this property are deemed broken.

Python defines several iterator objects to support iteration over general and specific sequence types, dictionaries, and other more specialized forms. The specific types are not important beyond their implementation of the iterator protocol.

Another important scripting item in Python is *Operators*. They are used to perform operations on variables and values. Python divides the operators into the following groups:

1. Assignment operators

2. Arithmetic operators

3. Logical operators

4. Comparison operators

5. Identity operators

6. Bitwise operators

7. Membership operators

Arithmetic operators are used with numeric values to perform common mathematical operations:[5]

Operator	Name	Example
+	Addition	x + y
-	Subtraction	x - y
*	Multiplication	x * y
/	Division	x / y
%	Modulus	x % y
**	Exponentiation	x ** y
//	Floor division	x // y

- **Python Assignment Operators:** Assignment operators are used to assigning values to variables:

Operator	Example	Same As
=	x = 5	x = 5
+=	x += 3	x = x + 3
-=	x -= 3	x = x - 3
*=	x *= 3	x = x * 3
/=	x /= 3	x = x / 3
%=	x %= 3	x = x % 3
//=	x //= 3	x = x // 3
**=	x **= 3	x = x ** 3
&=	x &= 3	x = x & 3
|=	x |= 3	x = x | 3
^=	x ^= 3	x = x ^ 3
>>=	x >>= 3	x = x >> 3
<<=	x <<= 3	x = x << 3

---

[5] https://docs.python.org/3/library/stdtypes.html, Python

- **Python Comparison Operators:** Comparison operators are used to comparing two values:

Operator	Name	Example
==	Equal	x == y
!=	Not equal	x != y
>	Greater than	x > y
<	Less than	x < y
>=	Greater than or equal to	x >= y
<=	Less than or equal to	x <= y

- **Python Logical Operators:** Logical operators are used to combining conditional statements:

Operator	Description	Example
and	Returns True if both statements are true	x < 5 and x < 10
or	Returns True if one of the statements is true	x < 5 or x < 4
not	Reverse the result, returns False if the result is true	not(x < 5 and x < 10)

- **Python Identity Operators:** Identity operators are used to comparing the objects, not if they are equal, but if they are actually the same object, with the same memory location:

Operator	Description	Example
is	Returns True if both variables are the same object	x is y
is not	Returns True if both variables are not the same object	x is not y

- **Python Membership Operators:** Membership operators are used to testing if a sequence is presented in an object:

Operator	Description	Example
in	Returns True if a sequence with the specified value is present in the object	x in y
not in	Returns True if a sequence with the specified value is not present in the object	x not in y

- **Python Bitwise Operators:** Bitwise operators are used to comparing (binary) numbers:

Operator	Name	Description
&	AND	Sets each bit to 1 if both bits are 1
|	OR	Sets each bit to 1 if one of two bits is 1
^	XOR	Sets each bit to 1 if only one of two bits is 1
~	NOT	Inverts all the bits
<<	Zero fill left shift	Shift left by pushing zeros in from the right
>>	Signed right shift	Shift right by pushing copies of the leftmost

Nonetheless, in the next part, we will give you more insight into how data types can be used, manipulated, and implemented in the Python world. We will also examine some useful functions and modifications to manipulate data sets. So, without wasting time, let's start with String data type.

STRING DATA TYPE

The most basic definition of string can be a sequence of characters, in which sequence is a data type that is made up of several elements of the same type, i.e., integers, float, characters, strings, etc. In Python, there is a unique code provided to all existing characters. The coding convention had been labeled as a Unicode format. It consists of characters of almost every possible language and emoticons too. Hence, strings can be considered as a special type of sequence, where all its elements are characters. For example, string "Hello, You" is basically a sequence ['H', 'e', 'l', 'l', 'o', ',', " ", 'Y', 'o', 'u'] and its length can be calculated by counting number of characters inside the sequence.

String handling in python requires the least effort because most string operations have very low complexity compared to other languages. There are several ways you can manage strings:

- **Concatenation:** Concatenation simply means to join two strings. Like to join "Hello" with "You," to make it "HelloYou." This is how you write it:

```
>>> print ("Hello" + "You");
```

A plus sign + is enough to complete the task. When used with strings, the + sign joins the two strings. Another example with multiple strings would be:

```
>>> s1 = "Name Python "
>>> s2 = "had been adapted "
>>> s3 = "from Monty Python"
>>> print (s1 + s2 + s3)
```

Result: Name Python had been adapted from Monty Python

- **Repetition:** In case, you want to write the same text multiple times on console, like repeat "Hey!" a 100 times you can always write it all manually, like "Hey!Hey!Hey!..." a hundred times or just do the following:

```
>>> print ("Hey!"*100)
```

So, if you want the user to input some number and based on that you want a text to be printed on console n times you can just create a variable n and use input() function to get a number from the user and then just multiply the text:

```
>>> n = input("Number of times you want
the text to repeat: ")
Number of times you want the text to
repeat: 4
>>> print ("Text"*4);
```

Result: TextTextTextText

- **Converting String to Int or Float datatype:** is also quite simple. There is a very common doubt amongst Python beginners that a number, when enclosed in quotes, becomes a string, and if you will try to perform mathematical operations on it, you will get an error.

```
numStr = '123'
```

In the statement above 123 is not a number, but a string. Thus, in such situation, to convert a numeric string into float or int datatype, we can use float() and int() functions.

```
numStr = '123'
numFloat = float(numStr)
numInt = int(numFloat)
```

With that, you can easily perform mathematical functions on the numeric value. And similarly, to convert an int or float variable to string, we can use the str() function.

```
num = 123
# so simple
numStr = str(num)
```

Slicing is another major string operation. Slicing allows you to extract a part of any string based on a start index and an end index. For instance, if we have a string and we want to extract a part of this string or just a character, then we can one of the following syntax:

- **string_name[starting_index: finishing_index: character_iterate]**

  - **String_name:** stands for the name of the variable holding the string.

  - **starting_index:** is the index of the beginning character which you want in your sub-string.

  - **finishing_index:** represents one more than the index of the last character that you want in your substring.

Python has a set of built-in methods that you can use on strings:[6]

- **str.capitalize():** Returns the copy of the string with its first character capitalized, and the rest of the letters are in lowercased.

- **string.casefold():** Returns a lowered case string. It is similar to the lower() method, but the casefold() – method converts more characters into lower case.

- **string.center():** Returns a new centered string of the specified length, which is padded with the specified character. The default character is space.

- **string.count():** Searches (case-sensitive) the specified substring in the given string and returns an integer indicating occurrences of the substring.

- **string.endswith():** Returns True if a string ends with the specified suffix (case-sensitive), otherwise returns False.

- **string.expandtabs():** Returns a string with all tab characters\t replaced with one or more space, depending on the number of characters before\t and the specified tab size.

- **string.find():** Returns the index of the first occurrence of a substring in the given string (case-sensitive). If the substring is not found it returns -1.

---

[6] https://www.tutorialsteacher.com/python/python-string, Python tutorials

- **string.index()**: Returns the index of the first occurrence of a substring in the given string.

- **string.isalnum()**: Returns True if all characters in the string are alphanumeric (either alphabets or numbers). If not, it returns False.

- **string.isalpha()**: Returns True if all characters in a string are alphabetic (both lowercase and uppercase) and returns False if at least one character is not an alphabet.

- **string.isascii()**: Returns True if the string is empty or all characters in the string are ASCII.

- **string.isdecimal()**: Returns True if all characters in a string are decimal characters. If not, it returns False.

- **string.isdigit()**: Returns True if all characters in a string are digits or Unicode char of a digit. If not, it returns False.

- **string.isidentifier()**: Checks whether a string is valid identifier string or not. It returns True if the string is a valid identifier otherwise returns False.

- **string.islower()**: Checks whether all the characters of a given string are lowercased or not. It returns True if all characters are lowercased and False even if one character is uppercase.

- **string.isnumeric()**: Checks whether all the characters of the string are numeric characters or not. It will return True if all characters are numeric and will return False even if one character is non-numeric.

- **string.isprintable()**: Returns True if all the characters of the given string are Printable. It returns False even if one character is Non-Printable.

- **string.isspace()**: Returns True if all the characters of the given string are whitespaces. It returns False even if one character is not whitespace.

- **string.istitle()**: Checks whether each word's first character is upper case and the rest are in lower case or not. It returns True if a string is titlecased; otherwise, it returns False. The symbols and numbers are ignored.

- **string.isupper()**: Returns True if all characters are uppercase and False even if one character is not in uppercase.

- **string.join()**: Returns a string, which is the concatenation of the string (on which it is called) with the string elements of the specified iterable as an argument.

- **string.ljust()**: Returns the left-justified string with the specified width. If the specified width is more than the string length, then the string's remaining part is filled with the specified fillchar.

- **string.lower()**: Returns the copy of the original string wherein all the characters are converted to lowercase.

- **string.lstrip()**: Returns a copy of the string by removing leading characters specified as an argument.

- **string.maketrans()**: Returns a mapping table that maps each character in the given string to the character in the second string at the same position. This mapping table is used with the translate() method, which will replace characters as per the mapping table.

- **string.partition():** Splits the string at the first occurrence of the specified string separator sep argument and returns a tuple containing three elements, the part before the separator, the separator itself, and the part after the separator.

- **string.replace():** Returns a copy of the string where all occurrences of a substring are replaced with another substring.

- **string.find():** Returns the highest index of the specified substring (the last occurrence of the substring) in the given string.

- **string.index():** Returns the index of the last occurrence of a substring in the given string.

- **string.rjust():** Returns the right-justified string with the specified width. If the specified width is more than the string length, then the string's remaining part is filled with the specified fill char.

- **string.rpartition():** Splits the string at the last occurrence of the specified string separator sep argument and returns a tuple containing three elements, the part before the separator, the separator itself, and the part after the separator.

- **string.split():** Splits a string from the specified separator and returns a list object with string elements.

- **string.rstrip()**: Returns a copy of the string by removing the trailing characters specified as argument.

- **string.split()**: Splits the string from the specified separator and returns a list object with string elements.

- **string.split lines()**: Splits the string at line boundaries and returns a list of lines in the string.

- **string.startswith()**: Returns True if a string starts with the specified prefix. If not, it returns False.

- **string.strip()**: Returns a copy of the string by removing both the leading and the trailing characters.

- **string.swapcase()**: Returns a copy of the string with uppercase characters converted to lowercase and vice versa. Symbols and letters are ignored.

- **string.title()**: Returns a string where each word starts with an uppercase character, and the remaining characters are lowercase.

- **string.translate()**: Returns a string where each character is mapped to its corresponding character in the translation table.

- **string.upper()**: Returns a string in the upper case. Symbols and numbers remain unaffected.

- **string.zfill()**: Returns a copy of the string with '0' characters padded to the left. It adds zeros (0) at the beginning of the string until the length of a string equals the specified width parameter.

SET DATA TYPE

Another Python's built-in data type could be characterized in the following way:

- The set data type has all its elements unique. It is not allowed to duplicate set elements.

- A set itself can be modified, but the elements contained in the set still remain of an immutable type.

- Sets are not ordered.

Nevertheless, it is very easy to work with sets in Python. You can create a set in two ways. First, you can define a set with the built-in set () function, to illustrate:

```
x = set(<iter>)
Or alternately, a set can be defined with
curly braces ({}):
x = {<obj>, <obj>, …, <obj>}
```

Many of the standard data operations that can be used for Python's other composite data types do not work the same way for sets. For example, sets cannot be indexed or sliced. But at the same time, Python provides a whole host of operations on set objects that generally imitate the operations that are defined for mathematical sets.

Operators and Methods

Most of the popularly requested set operations in Python can be performed in two different ways: by the operator or by a method. We can see how these operators and methods typically work, using set union as an example.

Given two sets, x1 and x2, the union of x1 and x2 is a set consisting of all elements in either set.

Consider these two sets:

```
x1 = {'food', 'bar', 'bass'}
x2 = {'bass', 'mouse', 'house'}
```
The union of x1 and x2 is {'food', 'bar', 'bass', 'mouse', 'house'}.

Make sure you notice that the element "bass," which appears in both x1 and x2, appears only once in the union because, as we have mentioned earlier, sets never contain duplicate values.

Another way set can be performed in Python is with the | operator:

```
≫ x1 = {'food', 'bar', 'bass'}
≫ x2 = {'bass', 'mouse', 'house'}
≫ x1 | x2
{'bass', 'mouse', 'house', 'bar', 'food'}
```

As an alternative, you can also obtain a set union with the. union() method. The method is brought on one of the sets, and the other is passed as an argument:

```
≫ x1.union(x2)
{'bass', 'mouse', 'house', 'bar', 'food'}
```

As you might have observed from the examples above, the operator and method behave almost identically. However, there is still a subtle difference between them. When you use the | operator, both operands must be sets. But the. union() method, on the other hand, will take any iterable as an argument, convert it to a set, and then perform the union.

Modifying a Set

And even though the elements contained in a set must be of the immutable type, sets themselves can indeed be modified. Like in the operations above, there is a mix of operators and methods that can be implemented to modify the contents of a set. Thus, each of the union, intersection, difference, and symmetric difference operators listed above has an augmented assignment form that can be applied to modify a set. And for each of them, there is a corresponding method as well:[7]

1. **x1.update(x2[, x3 …]); x1 |= x2 [| x3 …]:** Modify a set by union.

2. **x1.intersection_update(x2[, x3 …]); x1 &= x2 [& x3 …]:** Modify a set by intersection.

3. **x1.difference_update(x2[, x3 …]); x1 -= x2 [| x3 …]:** Modify a set by difference.

4. **x1.symmetric_difference_update(x2); x1 ^= x2:** Modify a set by symmetric difference.

5. **x.add(<elem>):** Adds an element to a set.

6. **x.remove(<elem>):** Removes an element from a set.

7. **x.clear():** Clears a set.

Frozen sets are also considered to be native data types in Python. And even if they have the same qualities of sets,

---

[7] https://realpython.com/python-sets/, Realpython

including class methods, they are immutable like tuples. In order to use a frozen set, call the function frozenset() and pass an iterable as the argument. And in case you pass another data type such as a list or string, frozen set will treat it as an iterable. And this means the value will be deconstructed into its individual parts, and later reduced to a set of unique immutable. To demonstrate:

```
myList = [1,1,2,3,4]
myString = "Hello"
frozenList = frozenset(myList)
frozenString = frozenset(myString)
print(frozenList) # frozenset({1, 2, 3, 4})
print(frozenString) # frozenset({'e', 'l', 'H', 'o'})
```

As you can see, frozen sets cannot be declared with a character notation like sets with curly braces, lists with square brackets, or tuples with parentheses. So, if you want to use a frozen set, you would have to use the function to script it. One might think that there is not much benefit in terms of performance when deciding to apply frozen sets. However, they could be of great value to construct more clear, concise code. Thus, by defining a variable as a frozen set, you are signaling other readers that they cannot modify this.

NUMBERS DATA TYPE

Python has many useful built-in data types that are extremely useful to understand if you want to write well-constructed code. Number data types store numeric values.

They are also considered immutable data types, so when you wish to change the value of a number, the data type results in a newly allocated object. Python variables can store different types of data, without the need to explicitly define a data type when the variable is created. Simply put, number objects are created only when you assign a value to them. For example:

```
var1 = 1
var2 = 10
```

Variable names in Python must stick to the following rules:

- Variable names only contain letters, numbers and the underscore character _.

- Variable names should start with a letter.

- Variable names cannot contain spaces or punctuation.

- Variable names should not be enclosed in any quotes or brackets.

Typically, Python supports four different numerical types:

- **int (integers):** sometimes also marked as ints, integers stand for positive or negative whole numbers with no decimal point.

- **long (long integers):** Could be referred to as longs, they are integers of unlimited size, written like integers but followed by an uppercase or lowercase L.

- **float (floating point real values):** Or just floats, they represent real numbers and are written with a decimal point dividing the integer and fractional parts.

- **complex (complex numbers):** are of the form a + bJ, where a and b are floats and J (or j) represents the square root of -1 (which is an imaginary number). Might also be worth mentioning that complex numbers are not used much in Python programming.

Integers

As stated earlier, the integer is a whole number, negative, positive or zero. In Python, integer variables are decided by assigning a whole number to a variable. Python's type() function can be used to define the data type of a variable:

```
>>> a = 2
>>> type(a)
<class 'int'>
```

The output <class 'int'> is the one that indicates the variable a is an integer. Integers can as well be negative or zero:

```
>>> b = -1
>>> type(b)
<class 'int'>
>>> z = 0
>>> type(z)
<class 'int'>
```

Floating Point Numbers

Floating-point numbers are another Python data type that is represented by decimals, positive, negative, and zero.

In addition, floats can also be represented by numbers in scientific notation, which contain exponents. When writing, afloat can be defined using a decimal point. when a variable is assigned. But to define floats in scientific notation, either a lower case e or an upper case E can be used:

```
>>> c = 6.2
>>> type(c)
<class 'float'>

>>> d = -0.03
>>> type(d)
<class 'float'>

>>> Na = 6.02e23
>>> Na
6.02e+23
>>> type(Na)
<class 'float'>
```

In case you want to define a variable as a float instead of an integer, even though the variable is assigned a whole number, a trailing decimal point. can be added. In this instance, however, a decimal point. comes after a whole number:

```
>>> g = 4
>>> type(g)
<class 'int'>
>>> f = 4.
>>> type(r)
<class 'float'>
```

Complex Numbers

Complex numbers are another useful numeric data type for problem solvers that are defined by using a real component + an imaginary component j. The letter j must be used to denote the imaginary component. If you use the letter i to define a complex number, Python is going to respond with an error.

```
>>> comp = 2 + 2j
>>> type(comp)
<class 'complex'>
>>> comp2 = 2+ 2i
        ^
SyntaxError: invalid syntax
```

Number Type Conversion

Python has the feature to convert numbers internally in an expression containing mixed types to a common type for evaluation. But, at times when you need to coerce a number explicitly from one type to another, you would have to add the following function parameters:[8]

- Type int(x) to convert x to a plain integer.

- Type long(x) to convert x to a long integer.

- Type float(x) to convert x to a floating-point number.

- Type complex(x) to convert x to a complex number with real part x and imaginary part zero.

- Type complex(x, y) to convert x and y to a complex number with real part x and imaginary party. x and y are numeric expressions.

---

[8] https://www.tutorialspoint.com/python/python_numbers.htm, Tutorialspoint

Moreover, Python has built-in functions that perform mathematical calculations (Mathematical Functions), functions that are commonly used for games, simulations, and testing (Random number functions), and ones that perform trigonometric calculations (Trigonometric Functions).

Python includes the following functions that perform **mathematical calculations:**[9]

1. **abs(x):** The absolute value of x: the (positive) distance between x and zero.

2. **ceil(x):** The ceiling of x: the smallest integer not less than x.

3. **exp(x):** The exponential of x: ex.

4. **fabs(x):** The absolute value of x.

5. **floor(x):** The floor of x: the largest integer not greater than x.

6. **log(x):** The natural logarithm of x, for x> 0.

7. **log10(x):** The base-10 logarithm of x for x> 0.

8. **max(x1, x2,...):** The largest of its arguments: the value closest to positive infinity.

9. **min(x1, x2,...):** The smallest of its arguments: the value closest to negative infinity.

10. **modf(x):** the fractional and integer parts of x in a two-item tuple. Both parts have the same sign as x. The integer part is returned as a float.

---

[9] https://www.tutorialspoint.com/python/python_numbers.htm, Tutorialspoint

11. **pow(x, y):** The value of $x^{**}y$.

12. **round(x [,n]):** x rounded to n digits from the decimal point. Python rounds away from zero as a tie-breaker: round(0.5) is 1.0 and round(-0.5) is -1.0.

13. **sqrt(x):** The square root of x for x > 0.

Random numbers that are mostly used for games, security, and privacy applications include the following functions:[10]

1. **choice(seq):** A random item from a list, tuple, or string.

2. **randrange ([start,] stop [,step]):** A randomly selected element from range(start, stop, step).

3. **random():** A random float r, such that 0 is less than or equal to r and r is less than 1.

4. **seed([x]):** Sets the integer starting value used in generating random numbers. Call this function before calling any other random module function. Returns None.

5. **shuffle(list):** Randomizes the items of a list in place. Returns None.

6. **uniform(x, y):** A random float r, such that x is less than or equal to r and r is less than y.

---

[10] https://www.tutorialspoint.com/python/python_numbers.htm, Tutorialspoint

Python includes the following functions that perform *trigonometric calculations:*[11]

1. **acos(x):** Return the arc cosine of x, in radians.

2. **asin(x):** Return the arc sine of x, in radians.

3. **atan(x):** Return the arc tangent of x, in radians.

4. **atan2(y, x):** Return atan(y/x), in radians.

5. **cos(x):** Return the cosine of x radians.

6. **hypot(x, y):** Return the Euclidean norm, sqrt(x*x + y*y).

7. **sin(x):** Return the sine of x radians.

8. **tan(x):** Return the tangent of x radians.

9. **degrees(x):** Converts angle x from radians to degrees.

10. **radians(x):** Converts angle x from degrees to radians.

LIST DATA TYPE

A list is the most basic data structure in Python that looks like a mutable, ordered sequence of elements. Any element or value that is inside of a list is called an item. And just as strings are defined as characters between quotes, lists are defined by those values that are placed between square brackets [ ].

Lists are particularly useful when you want to work with many related values, keep data together, condense your

---

[11] https://www.tutorialspoint.com/python/python_numbers.htm, Tutorialspoint

code, and perform the same methods and operations on multiple values at once.

The important characteristics of Python lists include the following:

- Lists are mutable.

- Lists are ordered.

- List elements can be accessed by index.

- Lists can be nested to arbitrary depth.

- Lists are dynamic.

When thinking about how someone might apply Python lists and other data structures that are types of collections, it is useful to try recalling all the different collections you might have in your possession: your personal files, your song playlists, your browser downloads, your email histories, the collection of videos you can access on a cloud service, and more. And with such lists, an ordered sequence of elements can become an item in a list and, therefore, be called individually, through indexing. In this case, lists are a compound data type that consists of smaller parts and are very flexible because they allow values to be added, removed, and changed. When you need to store a lot of values or iterate over values, and still be able to modify those values, you are most likely to need to work with list data types.

The list is the most versatile datatype available. The important thing about a list is that items in a list need not be of the same type, and can be written as a list of comma-separated values between square brackets.

Creating a list only requires putting different comma-separated values between square brackets. To demonstrate:

```
list1 = ['history', 'chemistry', 1993,
2019];
list2 = [1, 2, 3, 4, 5] ;
list3 = ["a", "b", "c", "d"]
```

Similar to string indices, list indices start at 0 and can be sliced, concatenated, and modified.

Accessing Values in Lists

In order to access values in lists, add the square brackets for slicing along with the index or indices to gather the value available at that index. For example:

```
Live Demo
#!/usr/bin/python

list1 = ['history', 'chemistry', 1993,
2019];
list2 = [1, 2, 3, 4, 5, 6, 7] ;

print "list1[0]: ", list1[0]
print "list2[1:5]: ", list2[1:5]
```

When the above code is executed, it produces the following result –

```
list1[0]: history
list2[1:5]: [2, 3, 4, 5]
```

Updating Lists

If you would like to update single or multiple elements, you should give the slice on the left-hand side of the assignment operator, and then just add elements in a list with the append() method. For example:

```
Live Demo
#!/usr/bin/python

list = ['history', 'chemistry', 1993,
2019];
print "Value available at index 2: "
print list[2]
list[2] = 2020;
print "New value available at index 2: "
print list[2]
```

When the above code is implemented, it should produce the following result:

```
Value available at index 2:
1993
New value available at index 2:
2020
```

Delete List Elements

To remove a list element, you can use either the del statement if you know exactly which element(s) you are deleting is placed, or apply the remove() method if you cannot locate it. For example:

```
Live Demo
#!/usr/bin/python

list1 = ['history', 'chemistry', 1993,
2019];
print list1
del list1[2];
```

```
print "After deleting value at index 2: "
print list1
```

When the above code is executed, it produces the following result:

```
['history', 'chemistry', 1993, 2019]
After deleting value at index 2:
['history', 'chemistry', 2019]
```

Basic List Operations

Lists respond to the + and * operators much like strings – concatenation and repetition, except that the result would be a new list, not a string.[12]

Python Expression	Results	Description
len([1, 2, 3])	3	Length
[1, 2, 3] + [4, 5, 6]	[1, 2, 3, 4, 5, 6]	Concatenation
['Hi!'] * 4	['Hi!', 'Hi!', 'Hi!', 'Hi!']	Repetition
3 in [1, 2, 3]	True	Membership
for x in [1, 2, 3]: print x,	1 2 3	Iteration

Built-In List Functions and Methods

Python includes the following list functions[13]

1. **cmp(list1, list2):** Compares elements of both lists.

2. **len(list):** Gives the total length of the list.

---

[12] https://www.tutorialspoint.com/python/python_lists.htm, Tutorialspoint
[13] https://www.python-ds.com/python-3-list-methods, Python DS

3. **max(list):** Returns item from the list with max value.

4. **min(list):** Returns item from the list with min value.

5. **list(seq):** Converts a tuple into list.

It also includes following list methods:

1. **list.append(obj):** Appends object obj to list.

2. **list.count(obj):** Returns count of how many times obj occurs in list.

3. **list.extend(seq):** Appends the contents of seq to list.

4. **list.index(obj):** Returns the lowest index in list that obj appears.

5. **list.insert(index, obj):** Inserts object obj into list at offset index.

6. **list.pop(obj=list[-1]):** Removes and returns last object or obj from list.

7. **list.remove(obj):** Removes object obj from list.

8. **list.reverse():** Reverses objects of list in place.

9. **list.sort([func]):** Sorts objects of list, use compare func if given.

DICTIONARY DATA TYPE

Dictionary in Python stands for an unordered collection of data values, used to store data values like a map. Unlike other data types that hold only a single value as an element, Dictionary holds key:value pair, which is added there mainly for optimization. However, keys in a dictionary do not allow Polymorphism (when the same method is declared multiple times, for multiple purposes, and different classes).

Creating a Dictionary

In Python, a Dictionary can be easily created by placing a sequence of elements within curly {} braces, separated by "comma." Typically, dictionary holds a pair of values, one of which would be the Key and the other corresponding pair element being its Key:value. Values in a dictionary can be of any data type and can be duplicated, whereas keys cannot be repeated and should be immutable. Additionally, dictionary keys are quite case sensitive, same name but different cases of Key would be treated distinctly.

Accessing Values in Dictionary

To access dictionary items, you can use the familiar square brackets together with the key to obtaining its value. To explain with a simple example:

```
Live Demo
#!/usr/bin/python

dict = {'Name': 'Mary', 'Age': 10, 'Class':
'First'}
print "dict['Name']: ", dict['Name']
print "dict['Age']: ", dict['Age']
```

When the above code is processed, it produces the following result:

```
dict['Name']: Mary
dict['Age']: 10
```

Updating Dictionary

A dictionary can be updated by simply adding a new entry or a key-value pair, which is going to modify an existing entry or delete an existing entry as shown in the simple example below:

```
Live Demo
#!/usr/bin/python

dict = {'Name': 'Mary', 'Age': 10, 'Class':
'First'}
dict['Age'] = 11; # update existing entry
dict['School'] = "High School"; # Add new
entry

print "dict['Age']: ", dict['Age']
print "dict['School']: ", dict['School']
```

When the above code is processed, it produces the following result:

```
dict['Age']: 11
dict['School']: High School
```

Delete Dictionary Elements

There are two options: you can either remove an individual dictionary element or clear the entire contents of a dictionary (which can be executed in a single operation). In order to explicitly remove an entire dictionary, you should use the del statement. Take a look at the following example:

```
Live Demo
#!/usr/bin/python

dict = {'Name': 'Mary', 'Age': 10, 'Class':
'First'}
```

```
del dict['Name']; # remove entry with key
'Name'
dict.clear(); # remove all entries in dict
del dict; # delete entire dictionary
print "dict['Age']: ", dict['Age']
print "dict['School']: ", dict['School']
```

Properties of Dictionary Keys

Normally, dictionary values have no restrictions – they can be of any arbitrary Python object, either standard objects or user-defined objects. Yet, the same is not true for the keys. There are two most important points to understand about dictionary keys:

1. More than one entry per key is not permitted. That means no duplicate key is allowed. And if duplicate keys were encountered during the assignment, the last assignment would win.

2. Keys must be immutable, meaning you can use strings, numbers, or tuples as dictionary keys, but something like ['key'] is not allowed.

Built-in Dictionary Functions & Methods

Python includes the following built-in dictionary functions:[14]

1. **CMP(dict1, dict2):** Compares elements of both dict.

2. **len(dict):** Gives the total length of the dictionary. This would be equal to the number of items in the dictionary.

---

[14] https://www.tutorialspoint.com/python/python_dictionary.htm, Tutorialspoint

3. **str(dict):** Produces a printable string representation of a dictionary.

4. **type(variable):** Returns the type of the passed variable. If a passed variable is dictionary, then it would return a dictionary type.

It also includes following dictionary methods:[15]

1. **dict.clear():** Removes all elements of dictionary dict.

2. **dict.copy():** Returns a shallow copy of dictionary dict.

3. **dict.fromkeys():** Create a new dictionary with keys from seq and values set to value.

4. **dict.get(key, default=None):** For key key, returns value or default if key not in dictionary.

5. **dict.has_key(key):** Returns true if key in dictionary dict, false otherwise.

6. **dict.items():** Returns a list of dict's (key, value) tuple pairs.

7. **dict.keys():** Returns list of dictionary dict's keys.

8. **dict.setdefault(key, default=None):** Similar to get(), but will set dict[key]=default if key is not already in dict.

---

[15] https://www.tutorialspoint.com/python/python_dictionary.htm, Tutorialspoint

9. **dict.update(dict2):** Adds dictionary dict2's key-values pairs to dict.

10. **dict.values():** Returns list of dictionary dict's values.

Tuple Data Type

Tuples are identical to lists in all respects, except for the following properties: they are defined by enclosing the elements in parentheses (()) instead of square brackets ([]); And unlike lists Tuples are immutable.

Tuple are usually preferred over lists in the following instances:

- Program execution is faster when manipulating a tuple than list.

- Tuple are used to prevent your data from being modified. If the values in the collection are meant to remain constant for the life of the program, using a tuple instead of a list secure the data type against accidental modification.

- A tuple can be used for instances when you want to use a dictionary data type, which requires as one of its components a value that is of an immutable type.

Creating a tuple only takes putting different comma-separated values. As an option, you can put these comma-separated values between parentheses also. To illustrate with an example:

```
tup1 = ('history', 'chemistry', 1993,
2019);
```

```
tup2 = (1, 2, 3, 4, 5) ;
tup3 = "a", "b", "c", "d";
```

The empty tuple is represented as two parentheses containing nothing –

```
tup1 = ();
```

To write a tuple containing a single value you need to add a comma, even though there is only one value:

```
tup1 = (60,);
```

Like string indices, tuple indices start at 0, and later can be sliced, concatenated, and modified.

Accessing Values in Tuples

To access values in tuple, you can use the square brackets for slicing along with the index or indices to get the value available at that index. For example:

```
Live Demo
#!/usr/bin/python
tup1 = ('history', 'chemistry', 1993,
2019);
tup2 = (1, 2, 3, 4, 5, 6, 7) ;
print "tup1[0]: ", tup1[0];
print "tup2[1:5]: ", tup2[1:5];
```

When the above code is executed, it produces the following result:

```
tup1[0]: history
tup2[1:5]: [2, 3, 4, 5]
```

Updating Tuples

As previously mentioned, tuples are immutable, which means you cannot update or advance the values of tuple elements. What you can do is to take portions of existing tuples to create new tuples, as the following example demonstrates:

```
Live Demo
#!/usr/bin/python

tup1 = (12, 34.56);
tup2 = ('abc', 'xyz');

# Following action is not valid for tuples
# tup1[0] = 100;

# So we shall create a new tuple as follows
tup3 = tup1 + tup2;
print tup3;
```

When the above code is executed, it produces the following result:

```
(12, 34.56, 'abc', 'xyz')
```

Delete Tuple Elements

It is not allowed to remove individual tuple elements. However, there seems to be nothing wrong with putting together another tuple with the undesired elements discarded. To explicitly remove an entire tuple, you should just use the del statement. For instance:

```
Live Demo
#!/usr/bin/python

tup = ('history', 'chemistry', 1993, 2019);
print tup;
```

```
del tup;
print "After deleting tup: ";
print tup;
```

This formula is going to produce the following result:

```
('history', 'chemistry', 1993, 2019)
After deleting tup:
Traceback (most recent call last):
    File "test.py", line 9, in
        print tup;
NameError: name 'tup' is not defined
```

Basic Tuples Operations

Tuples respond to the + and * operators much like strings; they mean concatenation and repetition here too, except that the result is a new tuple, not a string.[16]

Python Expression	Results	Description
len((1, 2, 3))	3	Length
(1, 2, 3) + (4, 5, 6)	(1, 2, 3, 4, 5, 6)	Concatenation
('Hi!',) * 4	('Hi!', 'Hi!', 'Hi!', 'Hi!')	Repetition
3 in (1, 2, 3)	True	Membership
for x in (1, 2, 3): print x,	1 2 3	Iteration

Built-in Tuple Functions

Python includes the following tuple functions –

1. **cmp(tuple1, tuple2):** Compares elements of both tuples.

2. **len(tuple):** Gives the total length of the tuple.

---

[16] https://www.tutorialspoint.com/python/python_tuples.htm, Tutorialspoint

3. **max(tuple):** Returns item from the tuple with max value.

4. **min(tuple):** Returns item from the tuple with min value.

5. **tuple(seq):** Converts a list into tuple.

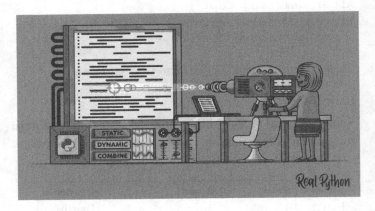

To conclude, effective data-driven science and computation require understanding of how data is utilized and manipulated. With this chapter, we attempted to outline and contrast how arrays of data are handled in the Python language itself, and how anyone can improve on this. In general, a data type is used to define the format, set the upper and lower bounds of the data so that a program could apply it appropriately. However, Python data types are created for much more than that. In Python, there is no need to declare a variable without explicitly mentioning the data type. Instead, Python determines the type of a literal directly from the syntax at runtime. This feature is also known as dynamic typing.

Dynamic typing is characteristic of many other scripting languages like Perl or PHP. It does indeed save you from writing "extra" lines of code, which, in turn, means less time spent writing code. Understanding this concept is fundamental to understanding much of the material throughout the rest of the book.

So by now, we have learned that data types are important because statistical methods and certain other things can only be used with a certain Python data type. You might be expected to analyze data differently and then categorize data; otherwise, it would result in a wrong analysis. Data types are essentially required to know what "kind" of data your variable holds or can hold. If you know this information in advance, you can save yourself from many runtime issues and utilize the minimum memory space.

## CHAPTER 3

Python Comments and Documentation

IN THIS CHAPTER

➤ Introducing main Python data types

➤ Talking about each type's in-built method descriptions

➤ Explaining how to access, update and modify Python data types

Each and every programming language has a concept called comments. Although comments do not change the outcome of a program, they still play an important role in programming. Comments are mostly used as statements that are ignored by the interpreter or compiler at runtime. Nevertheless, every coding language has its syntax, which

DOI: 10.1201/9781003229896-3

89

differentiates a comment from an actual code. Comments are a great way to improve the readability of your code, by explaining what you might want to be done in code in simple language.

Comments could also be beneficial during coding as the following functions:

- **Future reference:** Imagine that you have written a program that contains a few more hundred lines of code without any comments. If you open the program after one or two months, then you will find it challenging to understand your code. Moreover, you might even forget the role of a code block and would be forced to trace it again just to understand its intent. So putting a comment in code saves a lot of time when you know that you will have to come back to the code again.

- **Comments help to understand the code of others:** "No man is an island" and in most times we usually work in a team structure, having others review the code of one team member. Also, you might need to work on an item that was earlier worked on by your colleague. In both those cases, you will need to understand the code that someone else has scripted. If you have used comments in your code, it makes the other person's experience looking at your code much easier. He can complete a useful review, and also chances of defects are much lesser if someone else is editing your code.

- **Code debugging:** It happens sometimes that we need to check a part of the code to see whether it is working as expected or not. In this case, we can leave a comment on the remaining code. Without comments, we will have to go through removing the code to check the output and have to enter the same code again. This time-consuming process could be avoided by applying comments.

SINGLE LINE, INLINE, AND MULTILINE COMMENTS

Comments are useful information that the developers provide to make sure the reader can understand the source code. It is applied to explain the logic or a specific part of the code. Comments are particularly helpful to someone who is trying to maintain or enhance your code when you are no longer around to answer questions about it. These are often cited as useful programming techniques that do not take part in the output of the program but greatly improve the readability of the whole program.

As a rule, comments in Python begin with a hash mark (#) and whitespace character and continue to the end of the line. Typically, comments should look something like this:

This is a comment sample

Because comments do not contribute to execution, when you run a program, you will not see any indication of the comment there. Comments are meant to make code understandable for humans and are ignored by compilers.

In a "Hello, Reader!" program, a comment may look like this:

```
# Print "Hello, Reader!" to console
print("Hello, Reader!")
```

And since Python ignores everything after the hash mark and up to the end of the line, you can feel free to insert comments anywhere in your code, even inline with other code:

```
print("It is great work.") # There is a
mistake
```

When you run the above code, you will only see the output "It is great work." Everything else would be completely dismissed. Additionally, it is highly recommended to keep your comments short, concise, and to the point. And, while Python Enterprise Portal 8 (PEP 8) on "Style Guide for Python Code" advises writing code at 79 characters or fewer per line, it also suggests a maximum of 72 characters for inline comments and docstrings. In case your comment is going to exceed that length, then you will want to split it out over multiple lines.

In the same PEP 8 guide, Guido van Rossum adds a few remarks in regards to whitespace usage when commenting. To be precise, he states the following:[1]

- "Avoid trailing whitespace anywhere. Because it's usually invisible, it can be confusing: a backslash

---

[1] https://www.python.org/dev/peps/pep-0008/, Python

followed by a space and a newline does not count as a line continuation marker. Some editors don't preserve it and many projects (like CPython itself) have pre-commit hooks that reject it.

- Always surround these binary operators with a single space on either side: assignment (=), augmented assignment (+=, -= etc.), comparisons (==, <, >, ! =, <>, <=, >=, in, not in, is, is not), Booleans (and, or, not).

- If operators with different priorities are used, consider adding whitespace around the operators with the lowest priority. **Use your own judgment**; however, never use more than one space, and always have the same amount of whitespace on both sides of a binary operator."

Inline comments are applied on the same line as the statement, following the code itself. Just like other comments, they begin with a hash mark and a single whitespace character. Normally, inline comments look like this: [code] # Inline comment in regards to the code

The inline comments option should not be abused but can be effective for explaining complicated or non-obvious parts of code. They can also be helpful if you think you may not remember a line of the code you might need in the future, or if you are working in a collaboration with someone else who you know might not be fully informed with all aspects of the code. For instance, if you do not use a lot of math in your Python programs, you or your coding partner may not know that the following creates a complex number, so you might need to include an inline comment about that:

```
z = 4.5 + 7j # Create a complex number
```

Inline comments can also be applied to explain your logic behind doing something, or some extra information, as in:

```
x = 2 # Initialize x with an arbitrary
number
```

It has been a common practice for decades for the developers to add comments in the program in order to offer instructions on what the particular chunk of code is supposed to be doing when executed. In Python, only single-line comments that are made using "#" are accepted. And if you need to make a multiline comment, you should declare any symbol like declaring a variable in a function and call the function for entering plain text wherever it is needed in the program. Nevertheless, comments that are kept in line should be used only when necessary and when they can serve as helpful guidance for the person reading the program.

HOW PYTHON MULTILINE COMMENT WORKS?

Comments in the program could be viewed as a set of phrases meant to help users understand the program in the English language, attempting to make it somewhat readable. In Python, hash character (#) is used at the start of the line to make it a comment. There is no multiline comment concept in Python PEP 8 guide, but still, there is some description of triple quotes practice that could be declared as a multiline comment.

In Python, it is important to observe the alignment and the indentation method instead of placing curly braces for defining a function. Therefore, while writing the comments, we should be careful about indentation. For instance, if you add a note before function body but inside the function, which is also known as docstring, similar to multi-line comments that do not have any indentation. But, the function could have sets of code indented for multiple layers. So, you should properly indent comment indentation as well as function blocks.

It is safe to say that Python treats multiline comments as an ambiguity between online comments and docstring. As both multiline and docstring are applied within the triple quotes (" " " " " "). In python, comments are declared starting with the hash character (#) and ending with EOL – End of the line. And, docstring can be declared within triple quotes but within the function or module or method or class, which is similar to the multiline comment.

Block Comments

Block comments are generally applied to explain more complex code or sets of code that you do not expect your readers to be familiar with. These longer-form comments could be added to some or all of the code that follows, and are also indented at the same line as the code. In block comments, each line opens with the hash mark and a single space. In case you need to use more than one paragraph, they should be separated by a line that contains a single hash mark.

Here is an example of a block comment that defines what is happening in the main() function defined below:[2]

    # The main function will parse arguments via the parser
        variable. These

    # arguments will be defined by the user on the console.
        This will pass

    # the word argument the user wants to parse along with
        the filename the

    # user wants to use, and also provide help text if the user
        does not

    # correctly pass the arguments.

You should turn to block comments only when operations do not seem straightforward and are therefore demanding a better explanation. Otherwise, it is best to avoid over-commenting the code and try trusting other programmers to understand Python unless you are writing for a particular audience.

Shebang

Once you start reading Python scripts on your own, you might see that on some of them the first line opens with the #! characters and the path to the Python interpreter:

```
#!/usr/bin/env python3
```

This order of characters is called shebang and is used to tell the operating system which interpreter should be applied

---

[2] https://devguide.python.org/documenting/, Python

to parse the rest of the file. Scripts that start with shebang can be operated in the terminal without typing python before the script name. And since the shebang line starts with the hash character, it is also considered to be a comment and therefore is automatically ignored by the Python interpreter.

PYTHON COMMENTING BEST PRACTICES

An essential part of knowing how to write comments in Python is making sure that your comments are readable and easy to comprehend. We have collected a few tips to help you write better comments that could really support your code.

When Writing Code for Yourself

You can significantly make life easier for yourself by just properly commenting on your own code. Even if no one else will ever see it, you are going to work with it, and that is good enough reason to make it right. As a developer, one extremely useful way to use comments would be as an outline for your code. Especially when you are still halfway through scripting and not exactly sure how your program is going to turn out, then you can use comments as a tool to keep track of what is left to do, or even as a way of keeping the high-level flow of your program. For instance, you can use comments to outline a function in pseudo-code:

```
from collections import defaultdict

def get_top_companies(prices):
  top_companies = defaultdict(int)
```

```
# For each service range
  # Get company searches in price range
  then
  # Count num times company was searched
  # Take top 3 companies & add to dict

return dict(top_companies)
```

These comments will help you to plan get_top_companies(). And, once you know exactly what you want your function to do, you can work on translating that to code.

Using comments in this manner will help you to keep everything straight in your head. And as you glance through your program, you will know what is there left to complete in order to have a fully functional script. After translating the comments to code, make sure you remove previous comments that have become irrelevant so that your code stays clean and explicit.

You can also utilize the comments option as part of the debugging process. Try commenting out one of your old codes and see how that affects your overall output. If you agree with the change, then do not leave the code commented out in your program, as it might decrease readability. Instead, delete it and use version control in case you need to bring it back.

At last, you can apply comments to describe problematic parts of your own code. It usually happens that you put a project down and then have to come back to it months or years later. In this case, you will spend a lot of time trying to get reacquainted with what you scripted before. To avoid that, the best thing you can do is mark your thoughts and plans down so that it will be easier to get back up to speed later on.

When Writing Code for Others

People tend to skip and jump back and forth through text, the same applies to reading code. The only time one might be forced to read through the code line by line is when it is not working and you have to figure out what is the error about. In most other cases, you will take a quick look at variables and function definitions in order to get the idea. Having comments in simple English can really assist a developer to realize what is happening.

Therefore, try being nice to your fellow developers and use comments to help them grasp the purpose of your code. Inline comments should be used sparingly to clear up bits of code that are not definite on their own. And shall you have a complicated method or function that is not easily understandable; you may want to include a short comment after the def line to give some context to it:

```
def complicated_function(s):
    # This function is executing something
    complicated
```

This can help other professionals who are skimming your code to get an idea of what the function does. As for other public functions, you might want to include an associated docstring, whether it is complicated or not:

```
def sparsity_ratio(x: np.array) -> float:
    """Return afloat
```

This string will become the .__doc__ attribute of your function and will officially be associated with that specific method. The Python PEP 257 docstring guideline can help you to structure your docstring by offering sets of conventions that developers are most likely to use when structuring docstrings.

The PEP 257 guidelines also have conventions for multiline docstrings. These docstrings appear right at the top of a file and include a high-level overview of the entire script and what it is supposed to represent:

```
# -*- coding: utf-8 -*-
"""A module-level docstring
```

Docstrings do appear in the bytecode, so you can access this through the ``__doc__`` attribute. A module-level docstring like this one has to contain any essential or practical information for the developer reading it. When writing one as such, it is recommended to include all classes, exceptions, and functions as well as a one-line summary for each.

PYTHON COMMENTING WORST PRACTICES

Just as there are examples of good practices for writing Python comments, there are a few malpractices of comments that do not lead to decent Pythonic code. The following are just a few of them:

- **Avoid unconcise comments:** Your comments should be right to the point. In the case, where everything is plain understandable, you do not need to add anything. The acronym many developers use is D.R.Y., which stands for the programming slogan "Do not Repeat Yourself." This means that your code should be concise to the maximum. You do not need to comment on a part of code that sufficiently explains itself, like this one:

```
return x # Returns a
```

We can clearly see that x is returned, so there is clearly no need to repeat the statement in a comment. Malpractice as such makes comments W.E.T., meaning a developer "wrote everything twice." In addition, once you have set the code running, make sure to go back and remove comments that have become redundant.

- **Avoid unnecessary comments:** Unruly, complex comments can be a sign indicating that there might be a deeper problem with your code. Sometimes code comments could be used to mask the underlying errors of a program. Ultimately, comments should support your code, not try to hide miscommunications away. It is worth reminding yourself that if your code is poorly written, no amount of commenting is going to resolve it.

  A comment before every line should be kept simple by assigning obvious names to variables, functions, and collections. Your comments should rarely be longer than the code they back up. If you find yourself spending too much time and line space explaining what you did, then you need to go back and redesign to get a clearer code. In addition, using obvious naming conventions and removing all unnecessary comments can help to reduce the length of the code altogether.

- **Avoid rude comments:** It is very likely that you will be working on a development team project at some point in your life. And, when several people are all working on the same code, others are usually encouraged to come and review what you have written so far and give their honest feedback. From time to time, you might witness someone who dared to add a comment like this one:

```
# Re-write this one here to fix John's
stupid f** mistake
```

Simply put, it is not good to do this. Even if it is your friend's code and you are sure they will not be offended by it, it is still not acceptable. You never know what bits and pieces can slip to production, and how is it going to look if your client might accidentally discover it down the road. Including indecent and rude words in your comments is not the way to show that you are a professional.

Speaking of professional developers' ethics, it is worth mentioning that employees of tech organizations and companies (engineers, designers, and business executives) mainly based in the United States are choosing to sign The Never Again pledge to build solidarity and establish ground rules for IT infrastructure. By signing the pledge, they commit to:[3]

- We refuse to participate in the creation of databases of identifying information for the United States government to target individuals based on race, religion, or national origin.

---

[3] http://neveragain.tech/, The pledge

- We will advocate within our organizations:

  - To minimize the collection and retention of data that would facilitate ethnic or religious targeting.

  - To scale back existing datasets with unnecessary racial, ethnic, and national origin data.

  - To responsibly destroy high-risk datasets and backups.

  - To implement security and privacy best practices, in particular, for end-to-end encryption to be the default wherever possible.

  - To demand appropriate legal process should the government request that we turn over user data collected by our organization, even in small amounts.

- If we discover misuse of data that we consider illegal or unethical in our organizations:

We will work with our colleagues and leaders to correct it.

- If we cannot stop these practices, we will exercise our rights and responsibilities to speak out publicly and engage in responsible whistleblowing without endangering users.

- If we have the authority to do so, we will use all available legal defenses to stop these practices.

- If we do not have such authority, and our organizations force us to engage in such misuse, we will resign from our positions rather than comply.

- We will raise awareness and ask critical questions about the responsible and fair use of data and algorithms beyond our organization and our industry.

HOW TO PRACTICE COMMENTING?

The simplest way to start writing more Pythonic comments is just jumping straight to it.

You can start writing comments for yourself in your own code. Make it a task to include simple comments from now on where it is suitable. See if it adds more clarity to complex functions, and try putting a docstring at the top of all your scripts. Another good way to practice would be to go back and review any old codes that you have previously written. Observe where anything might not make sense, and tidy up the code. If it still needs some extra explanations, you might want to add a quick comment to help clarify the code's main resolution.

It is an especially good idea if your code is up on a provider of Internet hostings like GitHub that is used as a platform for software development and version control. Try reviewing your older work and help other people by guiding them through what you have already done.

Using the same platform, you can also give back to the community by commenting on other people's codes. If you ever find yourself downloading something from GitHub and later having troubles going through it, add comments as you come to understand how each piece of code can be optimized. After completing that, you can just sign your comment with your initials and the date, and then submit your changes as a pull request. If your changes are merged, you could be helping dozens if not hundreds of developers like yourself to get a better version of their projects.

To conclude, learning to comment well should be considered an extremely valuable tool. Not only can you learn how to write more clearly and concisely in general, but you will also no doubt gain a deeper appreciation of Python as well. Knowing how to write comments in Python can make life easier for many developers, starting with yourself. Well-placed comments can help to speed on what your code does, and also help you get re-acquainted with older codes of your own.

By noticing when you are applying comments to try and support poorly written code, you will be able to review and modify your code to make it more efficient. Commenting on previously written code, whether your own or another developer's, is a great option for those who are just starting to practice writing clean comments in Python. And, as you learn more about documenting your code, you can consider moving on to the next level which is code documentation.

PROGRAMMATICALLY ACCESSING DOCSTRINGS

As already pointed out in a previous section, Python code documentation is a key and continuous course in the process of software development. The term docstring is an abbreviation that stands for documentation string and defines your source code – what your function, module, or class does. As a rule, it is added as a regular comment right below the head of a code function, module, or method. Docstrings is a great way to create documentation for your Python code from within the code. This in-code documentation works for all modules, and all functions and classes exported by a module should also have docstrings. Public methods such as the __init__ constructor also have docstrings. A package may be documented in the module docstring of the __init__.py file in the package directory.

In order to write a docstring correctly, it is recommended to follow the official Python convention. In this case, PEP 257 – Docstring Convention written by David Goodger and Guido van Rossum himself, would be a great guideline to reflect upon. The aim of this PEP is to "standardize the high-level structure of docstrings: what they should contain, and how to say it."[4]

Single-Line Docstrings

Due to Python simplicity, the docstring comes as a single-line comment. However, keep in mind to start the text of a docstring with a capital letter, and end it with a period. Based on the trend that code is typically read more often

---

[4] https://www.python.org/dev/peps/pep-0257/, Python

than it is written, it is highly advised to describe what the documented structure does as a command, instead of explaining how it is done. Additionally, mentioning which kind of value is returned to the caller would also help to understand the result of the function or method.

And in regards to double-quotes, as long as both the beginning and the end quotes are similar, Python is quite progressive, and you are allowed to use three single quotes as well as three double-quotes. You just need to make sure that the closing quotes are in the same line as with the opening quotes. Besides, there is no need to add any empty lines before, or after the text of the docstring.

Multi-line Docstrings

Moreover, a docstring can as well be written as a multi-line comment. If you choose to use multi-line comments, two things are going to change – the encapsulation of the doc-string would be written in triple single- or double-quotes, and the structure of the docstring itself would get a deeper meaning assigned to the entire text.

The docstring of a script documents the script's function and command-line syntax together with other variables and files. You are allowed to be fairly elaborate (several screens full) when applying this docstring but at the same time make it as sufficient as possible for a new user to operate the command properly. It is also required to complete a quick reference to all options and arguments for an expert user.

The docstring for a module should typically list the classes, exceptions, and functions that are requested by the module, with a one-line summary of each. At the same time, docstring for a package __init__.py module is also expected to list the modules and sub-packages exported by the package.

The docstring for a function or method should summarize its behavior and list its return values, side effects, exceptions raised, and restrictions on when it can be applied. Optional arguments should be indicated, and keyword arguments that are part of the interface must be documented.

The docstring for a class should outline its behavior and list the public methods and other variables. If the class is supposed to be subclassed and has an additional interface for subclasses, this interface should be listed in the separate docstring. And, the class constructor should be documented in the docstring for its __init__ method.

If a class subclasses another class and its behavior is mostly obtained from that class, its docstring should mention this and outline the differences. You can use the verb "override" to indicate that a subclass method replaces a superclass method. And in addition to that, you can apply the verb "extend" to indicate that a subclass method calls the superclass method.

Docstring Formats

When it comes to docstrin formats, there is not just one binding setup. To be clear, there is more than one, and all of these format variants are compatible with multi-line docstrings.

- **reStructured Text (reST)/Sphinx:** This is considered to be the Official Python documentation standard that uses the syntax of the lightweight markup language reStructured text (reST).

- **Google Docstrings:** Google's style of docstring
- **NumPy/SciPy Docstrings:** A combination of reStructured text (reST) and Google Docstrings.

At the same time, there is a number of tools that auto-generate documentation and HTML documents from docstrings, such as Sphinx, Epydoc, Doxygen, PyDoc, pdoc, and the autodoc extension for Sphinx.

PyDoc, for instance, is a part of the Python distribution that gathers information about a module for the console, a web browser, or as an HTML document. In order to learn more about its module, function, class, or method, try looking inside the Python shell and using the help() function.

As mentioned earlier, Sphinx is the official Python documentation standard that is also used as a default generator for JetBrains' PyCharm integrated development environment. Basically, Sphinx style utilizes the syntax of a lightweight markup language reStructuredText (reST), designed to be both processable by documentation-processing software such as Docutils; and to remain easily accessible by human developers who are reading and writing Python source code.

Following PEP 257 guidelines for documentation is going to help you to understand the source code. And by applying the Sphinx tool, you would be able to automatically generate documentation from the docstrings in your code. Below we offer a simple step-by-step guide on how to easily auto-generate clean and well-organized documentation from Python code using Sphinx.

1. **Install Sphinx:** You can install Sphinx directly from a clone of the Git repository – https://github.com/sphinx-doc/sphinx. You can do it either by cloning the repo and installing from the local clone, on simply installing directly via git:[5]

```
git clone https://github.com/sphinx-
doc/sphinx
cd sphinx
pip install.
```

2. **Initialize the Sphinx Configuration:** In the root directory of your project, start sphinx-quickstart in order to initialize the sphinx source directory that enables a default configuration. Running this command will prompt you to fill out some basic configuration properties such as creating separate source and building directories, as well as indicating the project name, author name, and project version.

3. **Update the conf.py File:** The conf.py file located in the source folder describes the Sphinx configuration and controls how Sphinx builds the documentation. If you want to modify the theme, version, or module directory, you will need to insert these changes here. Below are a few standard overrides:

---

[5] https://www.sphinx-doc.org/en/master/usage/installation.html, Sphinx

- **Updating the Theme:** If you want to change the default theme for sphinx which is alabaster, you will find many other themes to choose from, and it is even possible to create your own. One of the popular themes is sphinx_rtd_theme, which is a modern and mobile-friendly theme. In order to install sphinx_rtd_theme, you will need to install the sphinx-rtd-theme Python package by running pip install sphinx-rtd-theme in the terminal.

- **Adding Extension Support for Autodoc:** The extensions variable is assigned to a list of extensions needed to build the documentation. For instance, if you're planning to include documentation from your doc using the autodoc directives, you will have to activate it by adding sphinx.ext.autodoc to the extension list. And if the documentation in your code follows the Google Python Style Guide, you will be expected to append sphinx.ext.napoleon to the extensions list.

  In addition to that, during each new Sphynx version release, it is recommended to update the documentation version to point to the project release version, either manually or using an automated process.

4. **Auto-Generate the rst Files:** Sphinx generates the HTML documentation from reStructuredText (rst) files. These rst files define each webpage and may contain autodoc directives, which are used to generate the documentation from docstrings in an automatic way. And since there is an automatic way to generate

these files, there is no need to manually type and file out the autodoc directives for each class and module. The sphinx-autodoc command is expected to automatically generate rst files with autodoc directives from your code. This command only needs to be run when a new module is added to the project.

5. **Build the HTML:** After you complete the configuration and rst files set up, you should be able to run the make HTML command from the terminal in the main directory to generate the HTML files. The HTML files will then be created inside the build/ HTML folder.

6. **Advanced Sphinx Items:** Make sure to note that there are additional Sphinx directives that can help your documentation look and feel more modern and organized. Here are some of the key features that can be useful for you to further customize the documentation. All examples are generated with the sphinx_rtd_theme:

   i. **Table of contents:** Sphinx uses a custom directive, known as the toctree directive, to describe the relations between different files in the form of a or table of contents.

   ii. **Warning box:** A warning box can be applied using the warning directive.

   For example: . . warning:: This is a **warning** box.

iii. **Image:** An image item can be added using the image directive.

iv. **Table:** Consequently, a table can be added using the table directive.

WRITE DOCUMENTATION VIA DOCSTRINGS

Python's documentation has for a long time been considered to be good for a free programming language. The reason for that was an early commitment of Python's creator,

Guido van Rossum, to provide documentation on the language together with its libraries, to the user community. So that they could actively participate in continuing involvement and assistance for creating and maintaining Python documentation.

Up to this day, community involvement takes many forms, from modifying bug reports to just plain criticizing when the documentation could be more polished or easier to use.

Moreover, there is a whole Index of Python Enhancement Proposals (PEPs) that go by the following categories:[6] Meta-PEPs (PEPs about PEPs or Processes), Other Informational PEPs, Provisional PEPs (provisionally accepted; interface may still change), Accepted PEPs (accepted; may not be implemented yet), Open PEPs (under consideration), Finished PEPs (done, with a stable interface), Historical Meta-PEPs and Informational PEPs, Deferred PEPs (postponed pending further research or updates) and finally, Abandoned, Withdrawn, and Rejected PEPs.

These documents are aimed at authors and potential authors of documentation for Python. More specifically, it is for users contributing to the standard documentation and developing additional documents using the same tools as the standard documents.

And in case you have an interest is in contributing to the Python documentation, but you do not have the time to learn all the PEPs related to a format for textual data and technical documentation – reStructuredText, then you can look it up further in this section. We are going to briefly introduce documentation concepts and syntax, intended

---

[6] https://www.python.org/dev/peps/#id6, Python

to provide authors with enough information to write documents productively.

Paragraphs

The paragraph is the most basic block in a reST document. They are simply parts of text separated by one or more blank lines. In Python indentation is significant, so all lines of the same paragraph should be left-aligned to the same level of indentation.

Inline Markup[7]

The standard reST inline markup is quite straight-forward:

```
one asterisk: *text* for emphasis
(italics),
two asterisks: **text** for strong emphasis
(boldface), and
backquotes: ``text`` for code samples.
```

Sections

Section headers are created by underlining or overlining the section title with a punctuation character. Generally, there should be no heading levels assigned to certain characters as the structure is determined from the succession of headings. But for the Python documentation, there is a suggested convention:[8]

```
# with overline, for parts
* with overline, for chapters
```

---

[7] https://devguide.python.org/documenting/, Python
[8] https://devguide.python.org/documenting/, Python

```
=, for sections
-, for subsections
^, for subsubsections
", for paragraphs
```

Sphinx brings a lot of new directives and interpreted text roles to standard reST markup. This section contains the reference material for these facilities. However, this material should be treated as just an overview of Sphinx's extended markup capabilities. Full coverage can be found in Python PEP documentations.

Meta-information Markup

The markup that is going to be described in this section is used to provide information about a documented module. Note that each module should be documented in its own file.

sectionauthor

Stands for the author of the current section. The element should include the author's name such that it can be used for presentation and email address. The domain name part of the address should be lower case. Example:

```
sectionauthor:Bill Gates <bill@gates.
org>
```

module

This mark stands for the beginning of the description of a module, package, or submodule. The name should be fully qualified and have short identifiers; examples that are in use include "IRIX," "Mac," "Windows," and "Unix." It is important to use a synopsis option that usually consists of one sentence describing the module's purpose – it is currently only used in the Global Module Index.

moduleauthor

The moduleauthor directive, which can appear multiple times, names the authors of the specific module code, just like sectionauthor names the author of a piece of documentation. It too does not result in any output.

In addition, it would be beneficial to make the section title of a module-describing file meaningful since that value will be inserted in the table-of-content of overview files.

Information Units

There is a variety of directives applied to describe specific features provided by modules. Each directive needs one or more signatures to provide basic information about what is being described, and the content should be the description. The standard version makes entries in the general index. However, if no index entry is desired, you can give the directive option flag: noindex:. The following example shows all of the features of this directive type:[9]

c:function

Describes a C function. The signature should be given as in C, for instance:

```
.. c:function:: PyObject* PyType_
GenericAlloc(PyTypeObject *type,
Py_ssize_t nitems)
```

---

[9] https://devguide.python.org/documenting/, Python

You will not have to backslash-escape asterisks in the signature; the names of the arguments should be given so they may be used in the description.

c:member

Describes a C struct member. Make sure that the text of the description includes the range of values allowed, how the value should be interpreted, and whether the value can be changed. References to structure members in text can use the member role.

c:macro

Stands for a "simple" C macro. To clarify, simple macros are macros that are used for code expansion, but which do not take arguments, therefore, cannot be described as functions. This is not to be used for simple constant definitions.

c:type

Describes a C type. The signature should just be the type name.

c:var

Describes a global C variable. The signature can as well include the type, such as:

```
.. c:var:: PyObject* PyClass_Type
```

data

Represents global data in a module, using both variables and values as "defined constants." Please note that class and object attributes are not documented using this directive.

exception

Characterizes an exception class. This signature can include parentheses with constructor arguments.

function

Describes a module-level function with parameters, and optional parameters in brackets. Default values can be given if it enhances clarity. For example:

```
.. function:: repeat([repeat=3[,
number=1000000]])
```

Typically, object methods as such are not documented using this directive. Bound object methods are placed in the module namespace as part of the public interface of the module and show information about side effects and possible exceptions.

coroutinefunction

Describes a module-level coroutine. A standard description is likely to include similar information to that described for function.

decorator

Classifies a decorator function. The signature should not represent the signature of the actual function, but the usage as a decorator. To illustrate with an example:

```
def removename(func):
    func.__name__ = ''
    return func

def setnewname(name):
    def decorator(func):
```

```
    func.__name__ = name
    return func
  return decorator
```

the descriptions should look like this:

.. decorator:: removename

Remove name of the decorated function.

.. decorator:: setnewname(name)
    Set name of the decorated function to *name*.

class

Classifies a class. The signature can include parentheses with parameters that will be displayed as the constructor arguments.

attribute

Describes an object data attribute. The description should include information about the type of data to be expected and whether it may be changed directly. This directive is usually nested in a class directive, like in the following example:

.. class:: Primary

However, it is also possible to document an attribute outside of a class directive, in case the documentation for different attributes and methods is split into multiple sections. The class name should then be included explicitly:

.. attribute:: Primary.social

method
> Describes an object method including similar information to that described for function. Nevertheless, the parameters should not include the self-parameter. This directive should be nested in a class directive, like in the previous directive above.

coroutinemethod
> Describes an object coroutine method including similar information to that described for function. However, the parameters should not include the self-parameter. This directive should also be nested in a class directive.

decoratormethod
> Same as a decorator, but for decorators that are methods. You may refer to a decorator method using the :meth: role.

staticmethod
> Describes an object static method. The description typically includes similar information to that described for function. This directive should as well be nested in a class directive.

classmethod
> Describes an object class method using similar information to that described for function. The parameters should not include the cls parameter and the directive should be nested in a class directive.

abstractmethod
> Describes an object abstract method including similar information to that described for function. This directive should be nested in a class directive.

<u>opcode</u>
Describes a Python bytecode instruction.

<u>cmdoption</u>
Stands for a Python command-line option or switch. Make sure option argument names are enclosed in angle brackets.

Inline Markup

As previously mentioned, Sphinx uses interpreted text roles to insert semantic markup in documents. The following roles relate to objects in modules and are possibly hyperlinked if a matching identifier is found:[10]

<u>mod</u>
The name of a module. Normally is dotted and used for package names.

<u>func</u>
The name of a Python function; dotted names may be used. In order to enhance readability, the role text should not include trailing parentheses. The parentheses are stripped when searching for identifiers.

<u>data</u>
The name of a module-level variable or constant.

<u>const</u>
The name of a "defined" constant. This may be a C-language #define or an immutable Python variable.

<u>class</u>
A class name; a dotted name may be used.

---

[10] https://devguide.python.org/documenting/, Python

meth

The name of a method of an object. The role text should include the type name and the method name.

attr

The name of a data attribute of an object.

exc

The name of an exception. A dotted name may be used. The name enclosed in this markup can include a module name and/or a built-in function of that name.

The following roles create cross-references to C-language if they are coded in the application programming interface (API) documentation:[11]

c:data

The name of a C-language variable.

c:func

The name of a C-language function should include trailing parentheses.

c:macro

The name of a "simple" C macro, as described above.

c:type

The name of a C-language type.

c:member

The name of a C type member.

---

[11] https://devguide.python.org/documenting/, Python

The following roles do not relate to objects, but are used to create cross-references or internal links:

envvar

An environment variable that is generated with index entries.

keyword

The name of a Python keyword. Using this role will result in generating a link to the documentation of the keyword.

option

A command-line option of Python. The leading hyphen(s) must be included. If a matching cmdoption directive exists, use simple ``code`` markup.

token

The name of a grammar token is mostly used in the reference manual to create links between production displays.

term

Reference to a term in the glossary. The glossary is created using the glossary directive containing a definition list with terms and definitions. It does not have to be in the same file as the term markup, but if you use a term that's not explained in a glossary, you'll get a warning during build.

command

The name of an OS-level command, such as rm. It does not do anything special except formatting the text in a different style.

dfn

Used to mark the defining instance of a term in the text without index entries generation.

file

The name of a file or directory. Within the building, you can use curly braces to indicate a "variable" part of content, for example:

```
``spam`` is installed in:file:`/usr/
lib/python2.{x}/site-packages …
```

Later in the documentation, the x will be displayed differently to indicate that it is to be replaced by the Python minor version.

guilabel

Labels presented as part of an interactive user interface must be marked using guilabel. This includes labels from text-based interfaces such as those created using curses or other text-based contents. Basically, any label used in the interface should be marked with this role, even button labels, window titles, field names, menu, and values in selection lists.

kbd

This role is used to mark a sequence of keystrokes. What form the key sequence takes usually depends on the platform- or application-specific conventions. In case, there are no relevant conventions, the names of modifier keys should be spelled out, in order to improve accessibility for new users.

mailheader
This markup does not imply that the header is being used in an email message, it is also used for headers defined by the various media type specifications. The header name should be entered in the same way it would normally be found in practice, with the camel-casing conventions being preferred where there is more than one common usage.

makeover
The name of a make variable.

manpage
A reference to a Unix manual page that also includes the section.

menuselection
Menu selections must be marked using the menuselection role. This is typically used to mark a complete sequence of menu selections, including selecting submenus and choosing a specific operation, or any subsequence of such a sequence. The names of individual selections should be separated by –>.

mimetype
The name of a media type or a major or minor portion of the media.

newsgroup
Stands for the name of a Usenet newsgroup.

program
The name of an executable program. This may differ from the file name for the executable for some

platforms. To be precise, you should drop the. exe (or other) extension for Windows programs.

<u>regexp</u>

A regular expression that does not include quotes.

<u>samp</u>

A piece of literal text, such as code. Within the contents, you can use curly braces to indicate a "variable" part, and if you don't need the "variable part" indication, you can use the standard ``code`` instead.

Now we are moving to the roles used to generate external links:[12]

<u>pep</u>

Refers to a Python Enhancement Proposal. This generates appropriate index entries. In the HTML output, this text is a hyperlink to an online copy of the specified PEP. However, such hyperlinks should not be a substitute for properly documenting the language in the manuals.

<u>rfc</u>

A reference to an Internet Request for Comments. This generates appropriate index entries in the HTML output, and this text is treated as a hyperlink to an online copy of the specified RFC. Note down that there are no special roles for including hyperlinks as you can use the standard reST markup for that purpose.

---

[12] https://devguide.python.org/documenting/, Python

The following paragraph-level markup directives are used to create short paragraphs and can be used inside information units as well as normal text:[13]

<u>note</u>

Used for an especially important bit of information about an API that a user should be aware of when using whatever bit of API the note is attached to. The content of this directive can be written in complete sentences and include all the necessary punctuation.

<u>warning</u>

An extremely important bit of information about an API that a user should be aware of when using whatever bit of API the warning is attached to. The content of the directive should also be written in complete sentences and include all appropriate punctuation. In the interest of not frightening users away from pages that are full of warnings as such, this directive should only be chosen over note for information in regards to the possibility of crashes, security hacks, and data losses.

<u>versionadded</u>

This directive comes with the version of Python that added the described feature, or a part of it, to the library or C API. When it applies to an entire module, it should be placed at the top of the module section before any prose.

<u>versionchanged</u>

Similar to versionadded, this directive describes when and precisely what changed in the named

---

[13] https://devguide.python.org/documenting/, Python

feature in some way (new parameters, changed side effects, platform support).

deprecated

Specifies the version from which the described feature is deprecated. Usually, there is one required argument that stands for the version from which the feature is deprecated. For example:. .deprecated:: 3.8

deprecated-removed

Similar to deprecated, but it additionally indicates from which version the feature is removed. With this directive, there are two required arguments: the version from which the feature is deprecated, and the version in which the feature is removed. For instance:.. deprecated-removed:: 3.8 4.0

seealso

Usually, sections need to include a list of references to structure documentation or external documents. These lists are created using the seealso directive. The directive itself is typically placed in a section just before any sub-sections. And for the HTML output, it is displayed boxed off from the main flow of the text. The content of the seealso directive should be a reST definition list. Example:

```
.. seealso::
 Module :mod:'zipfile'
 Documentation of the :mod:'zipfile'
standard module.

 'GNU tar manual, Basic Tar Format
<http://link>'_
```

```
Documentation for tar archive files,
including GNU tar extensions.
```

rubric

This directive is used to create a paragraph heading that are not included in the table of contents. It is currently used for the "Footnotes" caption.

centered

Using this directive, you can create a centered bold-faced paragraph.

substitutions

The documentation system offers three substitutions that are defined by default. They are placed in the build configuration file conf.py.

release

Replaced by the Python release the documentation refers to. Stands for the full version string, including alpha/beta/release candidate tags.

version

Replaced by the Python version the documentation refers to. And consists only of the major and minor version parts, e.g. 3.8

today

Replaced by today's date, or by the date set in the build configuration file. Normally has the following format – April 11, 2019.

Translating

There are separate Python documentation for translations that are strictly operated by the PEP 545 –

Python Documentation Translations. New versions are built by docsbuild-scripts and hosted on docs.python.org. There are several documentation translations already in production, and many others are still in progress:[14]

- Arabic (ar)
- Bengali as spoken in India (bn_IN)
- French (fr)
- Hindi as spoken in india (hi_IN)
- Hungarian (hu)
- Indonesian (id)
- Italian (it)
- Japanese (ja)
- Korean (ko)
- Lithuanian (lt)
- Polish (pl)
- Portuguese (pt)
- Portuguese as spoken in Brasil (pt-br)
- Russian (ru)
- Simplified Chinese (zh-cn)
- Spanish (es)

---

[14] https://www.python.org/dev/peps/pep-0545/, Python

- Traditional Chinese (zh-tw)
- Turkish (tr)

With Python, anyone can start a new translation. All you have to do is subscribe to the doc-sig mailing list, introduce yourself to the community and let everyone know about the translation you are starting. Afterwards, you should create the GitHub account and gather people to help you translate; otherwise, you will not be able to accomplish it on your own. You can use any tool to translate, as long as you can synchronize with Git version control system through Transifex or Github. Make sure you keep your fellow Pythonians updated about your work and progress via mailing list.

## CHAPTER 4

Programs, Algorithms, and Functions

IN THIS CHAPTER

➤ Reviewing main Python algorithms

➤ Discussing differences between Python Scripts and Modules

➤ Characterizing Python basic functions and Lambda functions

The standard data structures course, which introduces a collection of fundamental data structures and algorithms, can be taught on the basis of any programming languages available today. Nevertheless, most colleges and e-courses out there choose to adopt the Python language for introducing students to programming and problem-solving. Python provides several benefits over other languages such as C++ and Java, the most important of which is that it has a simple syntax that is easier to learn. In this chapter, we are going to expand upon the use of Python by providing Python-centric algorithms and functions for the data structures course. We shall learn about the clean syntax and powerful features of the language used throughout scripting and the underlying mechanisms of these features and their overall efficiency.

It is important to understand that the design and analysis of algorithms are a fundamental topic in computer science and engineering education nowadays. Unfortunately, traditional programming languages force many to deal with details of data structures and supporting routines, rather than algorithm design. Python represents an algorithm-oriented language that has been sorely needed in development. The advantages of Python include its uncomplicated syntax, the flexibility of basic functions, and interactivity that encourages experimentation. These and many other features we are going to analyze without further delay.

PYTHON SCRIPTS AND MODULES

In computing, the term script is used to refer to a file containing a logical sequence of orders or a set processing file. This usually comes as a simple program that is stored in a plain text file. Thus, a plain text file containing Python code that is designed to be directly executed by the user is called script, an informal term that means a top-level program file. On the other hand, a plain text file containing Python code that is created to be imported and used from another Python file is what we call a module. The main difference between a module and a script is that modules are meant to be imported, while scripts are made to be directly executed. In any case, the important thing is to learn how to run the Python code you write into your modules and scripts. And scripts are always processed by an interpreter, which is responsible for executing each command sequentially.

What's the Python Interpreter?

Python is an excellent programming tool that allows you to be productive in a wide variety of ways. Python also has a piece of software called an interpreter. The interpreter is the program you are going to need to run Python code and scripts properly. In technical terms, the interpreter is a layer of software that operates between your program and computer hardware to get your code running. Depending on the code implementation you use, the interpreter can be:

- A program written in Python itself usually uses PyPy interpreter.

- A program written in C run with CPython, which is the core implementation of the language.

- A program written in Java operates with Jython.

- A program implemented in .NET, usually use an open-source IronPython interpreter.

Given examples of interpreters are able to run Python code in two different ways: as a script or module or alternatively as a piece of code scripted into an interactive session. Nevertheless, whatever form the interpreter can take, the code you write will have to be run by this program. Therefore, the first condition to be able to implement Python scripts is to have the interpreter correctly installed on your system.

When you start to run Python scripts, a multi-step process sets in motion. In this process, the interpreter will:

- Process all the statements of your script in sequential order.

- Compile the source code to an intermediate format, also known as bytecode.

   This bytecode in this case is used as a translation tool of the code into a lower-level language that could be platform-independent. Its main purpose is to optimize code realization. So, the next time the interpreter runs your code, it will bypass this compilation process. To put it simply, this code optimization is only necessary to proceed with modules or other imported files, and not with executable scripts.

- Send away the code for execution.

   At this step, something known as a Python Virtual Machine (PVM) comes into play. The PVM is the runtime engine that is used for iteration over the instructions of your bytecode to test and run them one by one. The PVM is not just a separate component of Python, it is an essential part of the Python system you need to install on your machine. Technically, the PVM is the last step of what is called the Python interpreter.

The whole course to run Python scripts is known as the Python Execution Model. In addition, there are many other ways to run Python scripts:

Using the Python Command

Python command is the most basic and practical way to run Python scripts. All you need to do to run Python scripts with the python command is to open a command-line and type in the word python, or python3 if you have both versions, followed by the path to your script. To illustrate:

```
$ python3 hello.py
Hello There!
```

If everything works fine, then after you press Enter, you will be able to see the phrase Hello There! on your screen. With these simple steps, you have just run a Python script. But in case, if it does not work right, it is recommended to check your system PATH, your Python installation, the way you created the hello.py script, space where you saved it.

At times, it is also useful to save the output of a script for later analysis. You can do it in the following manner:

```
$python3 hello.py > output.txt
```

This operation redirects the output of your script to output.txt, rather than to the standard system output (stdout). The process is also known as stream redirection and is available on both Windows and Unix-like systems. If output.txt does not exist, then it's automatically created. On the other hand, if the file already exists, then its contents will be replaced with the new output.

Consequently, if you want to add the output of consecutive executions to the end of output.txt, then you must use two angle brackets (≫) instead of one, just like this:

```
$ python3 hello.py ≫ output.txt
```

Using the Script Filename

On recent versions of Windows, it is convenient to run Python scripts by simply entering the name of the file containing the code at the command space:

```
C:\devspace> hello.py
Hello There!
```

This procedure is possible because Windows has the system registry and the file association to assign which program to use for running a particular file. On Unix-like systems, such as GNU/Linux, you can achieve something similar by adding a first line with the text #!/usr/bin/env python, just as you do with hello.py.

For Python, this translates as a simple comment, but this line indicates what program must be activated to run the file for the operating system. This line opens with the #! character combination, which is commonly called hashbang or shebang and continues with the path to the interpreter. There are two ways to specify the path to the interpreter:

#!/usr/bin/python: used to script the absolute path.

#!/usr/bin/env python: for when you are using the operating system env command, which locates and implements Python by searching the PATH environment variable.

This last option is useful for Unix-like systems to locate the interpreter in different places. Eventually, to execute a script like this one, you need to assign execution permissions to it and then type in the filename at the command line.

How to Run Python Scripts Interactively

It is also feasible to run Python scripts and modules from an interactive session. This possibility offers you a variety of possibilities. When you take advantage of importing a module, you can load its contents for later access and use. The interesting point about this process is that import runs the code as its final step.

If the module contains only classes, functions, variables, and constants definitions, you probably will not be able to track if the code was actually run, but when the module includes calls to functions, methods, or other statements that generate visible results, then you will be able to observe its execution. This provides you with another option to run Python scripts:

```
>>> import hello
Hello There!
```

You should take note that this option works only once per session. After the first import, successive import executions will be of no use, even if you modify the content of the module. This is because import operations are expensive and could run only once. To illustrate with an example:

```
>>> import hello  # Do nothing
>>> import hello  # Do nothing again
```

These two import operations do nothing because Python knows that hello has already been imported. However, there are some requirements for this method to work – firstly, the file with the Python code must be located in your current working directory. And secondly, the file should be in the Python Module Search Path (PMSP), where Python can look for the modules and packages you import.

How to Run Python Scripts from an IDE or a Text Editor

When scripting larger and more complicated applications, it is recommended that you use an integrated development environment (IDE) or an advanced text editor. Most of these programs have the capacity to run your scripts from inside the environment itself. It is common for them to include a Run or Build command, which is usually available from the toolbar or from the main menu.

Python's standard distribution package already includes IDLE as the default IDE, and you can use it to write, debug, modify, as well as to run your modules and scripts. Other IDEs such as Eclipse-PyDev, PyCharm, Eric, and NetBeans also let you run Python scripts from inside the environment. In addition, you also have advanced text editors like

Sublime Text and Visual Studio Code that also allow you to run your scripts.

How to Run Python Scripts from a File Manager

Running a script simply by double-clicking on its icon in a file manager is another easy way to run your Python scripts. This option may not be widely popular in the development stage, but it may be useful when you are ready to release your code for production. However, in order to be able to run your scripts with a double-click; you should satisfy some conditions that will depend on your operating system.

Windows, for instance, associates the extensions .py and .pyw with the programs python.exe and pythonw.exe. This allows you to run your scripts by double-clicking on them. And when you have a script with a command-line interface, it is likely that you only see the flash of a black window on your screen. To avoid this from happening, you can add a statement like input('Press Enter to Continue…') at the end of the script. And this way, the program will not process further until you press Enter. Nonetheless, if your script has any error, the execution will be aborted before reaching the input() statement, and you still will not be able to watch the result.

On Unix-like systems, you will be able to run your scripts by double-clicking on them in your file manager by applying the shebang variable that we have mentioned before. Likewise, you may not notice any results on screen when it comes to command-line interface scripts.

And since the execution of scripts through double-click has several limitations and usually depends on many factors such as the operating system, the file manager, execution permissions, and file associations, it is highly advised that you see it as a viable option for scripts already debugged and ready to go into production.

In addition, if you do not know where to start, you can take a look at the following five most popular scripts in Python: joining two strings, floating-point in the string, raising a number to a power, working with Boolean types, applying If else statement and making use of AND and OR operators.

Joining Two Strings

There are many ways to join string values in python. Yet, the most simple way to combine two string values in python is to use the '+' operator. In this case, two string values are assigned in two variables, and another variable is used to store the joined values that are printed later.

```
string1 = "Hello"
string2 = "World"
joined_string = string1 + string2
print(joined_string)
```

The following output will appear after running the script from the editor. As a result, two words, "Hello" and "World" are joined, and "HelloWorld" is printed as output.

Format Floating Point in the String

Floating point number is required in programming for making up fractional numbers, and sometimes it takes formatting the floating-point number for programming purposes. String formatting and string interpolation are used in the following script to format a floating-point number.

format() method with format width is used in string formatting, and "%" symbol with the format with width is used in string interpolation. According to the formatting width, 5 digits are set before the decimal point, and 2 digits are set after the decimal point.[1]

```
# Use of String Formatting
float1 = 563.78453
print("{:5.2f}".format(float1))

# Use of String Interpolation
float2 = 563.78453
print("%5.2f" % float2)
```

The following output will be available after running the script from the editor.

Raise a Number To a Power

In the following script, three ways are displayed to calculate the xn in Python. Double '*' operator, pow() method, and math.pow() method are used for calculating the xn. The values of x and n are initialized with numeric values. Double '*' and pow() methods are used for calculating the power of integer values. math.pow() can calculate the power of fractional numbers; also, that is shown in the last part of the script.[2]

```
import math
# Assign values to x and n
x = 4
n = 3
```

---

[1] https://linuxhint.com/python_scripts_beginners_guide/#post-67157-02, Python

[2] https://linuxhint.com/python_scripts_beginners_guide/#post-67157-02, Python

```
# Method 1
power = x ** n
print("%d to the power %d is %d" %
(x,n,power))

# Method 2
power = pow(x,n)
print("%d to the power %d is %d" %
(x,n,power))

# Method 3
power = math.pow(2,6.5)
print("%d to the power %d is %5.2f" %
(x,n,power))
```

The following output will appear after running the script. The first two outputs will have the result of 43, and the third output will show the result of 26.5.

Working with Boolean Types

The different uses of Boolean types are shown in the following script. The first output will print the value of val1 that contains the Boolean value, true. All positive are negative numbers return true as Boolean value and only zero returns false as a Boolean value. Hence, the second and third outputs will print true for positive and negative numbers. The fourth output will print false for 0, and the fifth output will print false because the comparison operator returns false.[3]

```
# Boolean value
val1 = True
print(val1)
```

---

[3] https://linuxhint.com/python_scripts_beginners_guide/#post-67157-02, Python

```
# Number to Boolean
number = 7
print(bool(number))

number = -10
print(bool(number))

number = 0
print(bool(number))

# Boolean from comparison operator
val1 = 4
val2 = 6
print(val1 < val2)
```

The following output will appear after running the script.

Use of If-Else Statement

The following script is used to create a conditional statement in python. The declaration of the if-else statement in python is different than other languages – no curly brackets are required to define the if-else block in python like other languages, but the indentation block must be added properly other the script will show an error. A colon(:) is used after the 'if' and 'else' block to define the starting of the block.

```
# Assign a numeric value
number = 77

# Check the is more than 77 or not
if (number >= 77):
    print("You have passed")
else:
    print("You have not passed")
```

The following output will appear after running the script.

Use of AND and OR Operators

The following script applied to AND and OR operators in the conditional statement. AND operator returns true when the two conditions return true, and OR operator returns true when any condition of two conditions returns true. Two floating-point numbers will be taken as MCQ and theory marks.

```
# Take MCQ marks
mcq_marks = float(input("Enter the MCQ
marks: "))
# Take theory marks
theory_marks = float(input("Enter the
Theory marks: "))

# Check the passing condition using AND
and OR operator
if (mcq_marks >= 20 and theory_marks >=
10) or (mcq_marks + theory_marks) >=30:
    print("\nYou have passed")
else:
    print("\nYou have failed")
```

Modules or Modular programming stand for the process of breaking a large, complex programming task into separate, smaller subtasks or modules. Individual modules can then be piled together like building bricks to create another application. There are multiple advantages to modularizing code when it comes to larger application:

- **Simplicity:** Rather than focusing on the entire problem at hand, a module allows you to focus on one small portion of the problem. And if you are working on a single module, you know you have a smaller problem domain to tackle first. This makes overall development manageable and less error-prone.

- **Maintainability:** Modules are typically designed to create logical boundaries between different problems and tasks. If modules are written to minimize interdependency, there is a decreased possibility that modifications to a single module will impact other bits of the program. This way, you might even be able to make changes to a module without having any knowledge of the script outside that module. This makes it more convenient for a team of many developers to work in collaboration on a large application.

- **Reusability:** Functionality defined in a single module can be easily reused through an appropriately defined interface. With that, there is no need to duplicate your codes.

- **Organizing:** Modules usually define a separate namespace, which helps prevent any collisions between identifiers to happen.

Typically, there are three different ways to define a module in Python: a module can be written in Python itself; it can be written in C and loaded dynamically at run-time, or a built-in module could intrinsically be contained in the interpreter. Nevertheless, a module's contents are accessed the same way in all three cases via the import statement. Module contents are made available to the caller with the import statement as shown below:

```
import <module_name>
```

This is the simplest that does not make the module contents directly accessible to the caller. Each module has its own private symbol table, which also serves as the global symbol table for all objects defined in the module. Thus, it also lets a module create a separate namespace, as previously noted.

Locating Modules

When you import a module, the Python interpreter searches for the module in the current directory. And in case the module is not found, Python then searches each directory in the shell variable PYTHONPATH. If that fails too, Python checks the default path. On UNIX, this default path is normally/usr/local/lib/python/.

To be precise, the module search path is stored in the system module sys as the sys.path variable. The sys.path variable contains the current directory, PYTHONPATH, and the installation-dependent default. The PYTHONPATH is an environment variable, consisting of a list of directories and the syntax of PYTHONPATH is similar to that of the shell variable PATH.

Here is the common PYTHONPATH from a Windows system –

```
set PYTHONPATH = c:\python20\lib;
```

And here is the basic PYTHONPATH from a UNIX system –

```
set PYTHONPATH = /usr/local/lib/python
```

Standard Modules

Python comes with a library of standard modules, described in a separate document, also known as the Python Library

Reference. Some modules that are built into the interpreter provide access to operations that are not part of the core of the language but are nevertheless necessary for efficiency or to provide access to operating system functions such as system calls. The set of such modules is a configuration option that highly depends on the underlying platform. One module, in particular, sys is built into every Python interpreter. The variables sys.ps1 and sys.ps2 define the strings used as primary and secondary prompts:

```
>>>
>>> import sys
>>> sys.ps1
'>>>'
>>> sys.ps2
'...'
>>> sys.ps1 = 'C>'
C> print('Yes!')
Yes!
C>
```

Python Packages

It often happens that you develop a very large application that includes many modules. As the number of modules grows, it becomes challenging to keep track of them all, especially if they are stored in one location. This is particularly difficult if they have similar names or functionality means. In this case, you might wish for a tool or system to be able to group and organize them.

Packages enable hierarchical structuring of the module namespace through dot notation. In the same way that modules help avoid confusion between variable names, packages help avoid confusion between module names. Creating a package is a straightforward process that makes use of the operating system's default hierarchical file structure.

To demonstrate, let's imagine you need to design a collection of modules for the uniform handling of sound files and sound data. And since there are many different sound file formats, you may need to create and maintain a growing collection of modules for the conversion between the various file formats. There are also many different operations you might want to perform on sound data, such as mixing, adding echo, applying an equalizer function, creating a stereo effect, so in addition, you will be scripting a stream of modules to perform these operations. Here's a possible structure for your package designed in terms of a hierarchical filesystem:[4]

```
sound/          Top-level package
    __init__.py  Initialize the sound package
    formats/     Subpackage for file format
conversions
        __init__.py
        wavread.py
        wavwrite.py
        aiffread.py
        aiffwrite.py
        auread.py
        auwrite.py
        ...
    effects/     Subpackage for sound effects
        __init__.py
```

4 https://docs.python.org/3/tutorial/modules.html, Python

```
      echo.py
      surround.py
      reverse.py
      ...
filters/          Subpackage for filters
      __init__.py
      equalizer.py
      vocoder.py
      karaoke.py
```

PYTHON ALGORITHMS

Algorithms are rules or instructions that are structured in a finite order to solve problems and obtain the required results. They also used to give the pseudocode for problems and can be applied in several languages as they are not considered to be language-specific.

How Do You Write Algorithms?

Algorithms are generally written as a combination of user-friendly language and a few common programming languages. They are typically written down in steps. However, there are no distinct rules to form algorithms but you will need to keep the following points in mind:

- Point out what is the exact problem
- Define where you want to start
- Determine where you need to stop
- Decide on the intermediate steps
- Review your algorithm steps

For example, if you have to formulate an algorithm to check if an expert has passed a qualification exam or not, you can follow the given steps:

Step 1: START

Step 2: Define two variables x, y

Step 3: Store the marks obtained by the expert in x

Step 4: Store the minimum passing score in y

Step 5: Check if x is greater than or equal to y. If yes, then return "Pass" else return "Fail"

Step 6: STOP

Nevertheless, you may manipulate the steps according to your needs and preferences. For example, you can assign the values to the variables in step 2 itself rather than taking steps 3 and 4. This way, a single problem can have multiple solutions, and it depends on the problem and the programmer to choose the most practical solution.

Characteristics of an Algorithm

However, not all procedures can be treated as an algorithm. An algorithm should have the following characteristics:

- **Unambiguous:** Algorithm should be clear and have transparent order of steps (or phases), with an understandable set of inputs/outputs that lead to only one meaning.

- **Input:** An algorithm should have 0 or more well-established inputs.

- **Output:** An algorithm should have 1 or more well-explained outputs and should match the desired output.

- **Finiteness:** Algorithms must end after a certain number of steps.

- **Feasibility:** Should be viable with the available resources.

- **Independent:** An algorithm should have marked out step-by-step directions, which should not depend on any programming code.

From the data structure point of view, there are certain categories of algorithms that are of utmost importance:

- **Search:** Algorithm that helps to search an item in a data structure.

- **Sort:** Algorithm that is used to sort items in a certain order.

- **Insert:** Algorithm to insert items in a data structure.

- **Update:** Algorithm applied to update an existing item in a data structure.

- **Delete:** Algorithm that deletes an existing item from a data structure.

Algorithms may be perceived as paradigms or strategies for solving problems. There are two most common algorithmic paradigms are brute force and divide & conquer.

Brute Force

Brute force algorithms are great methods of solving a problem through exercising computing power and testing all possibilities to find a solution rather than using a more advanced strategy to advance overall tactics efficiency.

For instance, if you are trying to figure out a four-digit password combination application of the brute force approach would let you test every possible combination of four-digit numbers from 0000 to 9999. Linear search, a method to find a target value using a specific list, is an example of the brute force method. The search algorithm will pass through the array and check each element until a match is found. The advantage of using the brute force method is that you are definitely guaranteed to find the solution. It is also pretty straightforward and easy to implement compared to other more complicated algorithmic strategies. On the other hand, even though it is easy to implement, it is also the most inefficient solution. It makes it challenging to improve performance or find possible shortcuts with this strategy.

Divide and Conquer

Divide and conquer is another algorithmic paradigm that enables solving a problem by dividing it into smaller sub-problems. Once the sub-problems are small enough, they will each be solved separately. And in the end, the algorithm repeatedly combines the solved sub-solutions into a solution for the original problem. It's very efficient and fast when dealing with general case solutions where the problem can easily be divided into sub-problems. It is also preferable in terms of memory usage, as dividing the problems into micro sub-problems allows the problem to be solved in the cache itself. However, due to its recursive approach, it may be quite slow. There is also a possibility that the approach might duplicate sub-problems leading to large recursive sets, which will consume extra space.

Moving ahead with these Data Structures and Algorithms in Python, we should take a closer look at some of the important algorithms such as the Tree Traversal Algorithms, Searching Algorithms, and Sorting Algorithms.

Tree Traversal Algorithms

Trees in Python are non-linear data structures that require visiting each node present in the tree exactly once in order to update or check them. Based on the order in which the nodes are visited, there can be three types of tree traversals: pre-order traversal (Root-Left-Right), in-order traversal (Left-Root-Right), and post-order traversal (Left-Right-Root).

In-order Traversal   In-order traversal stands for traversing the tree in such a way that you first visit the left nodes followed by the root and then right nodes. You start your traversal from all the nodes in the left subtree, moving towards the root and finally getting to the right subtree. The algorithm for In-order traversal looks like this:

Step 1: Traverse through the nodes present in the left subtree

Step 2: Check the root node

Step 3: Traverse the right subtree.

Pre-order Traversal   In a Pre-Order traversal, the root node is visited first, followed by the left subtree and then the right subtree. The algorithm for Pre-order traversal will be the following:

Step 1: Visit the root node

Step 2: Traverse through the nodes present in the left subtree

Step 3: Traverse the right subtree.

Post-order Traversal   Post-order traversal starts with the left then to the right, and only then, the root. The algorithm for Post-order traversal will be as follow:

Step 1: Traverse through the nodes present in the left subtree

Step 2: Traverse the right subtree

Step 3: Visit the root node.

Sorting Algorithms

Sorting of data should be considered as a real-time problem that requires a number of sorting algorithms to be solved. And in this case, sorting algorithms are used to sort data into the requisite order. Sorting algorithms can be divided into five types that are:

- Merge Sort

- Bubble Sort

- Insertion Sort

- Selection Sort

Merge Sort   Merge Sort algorithm operates based on the Divide and Conquer rule. With that, the given list of items is first divided into smaller lists until it reaches a point where each list has exactly one item. By default, a list consisting of one item will be sorted, and the merge sort algorithm then compares lists and reorders them in the sequence. This process is done recursively until it reaches a stage where there is only one, sorted list. To simplify, the Merge Sort Algorithm might look like this:

Step 1: Check if the list contains more than one items; if yes, divide the list into two lists, else the list is sorted

Step 2: The list is to be divided repeatedly until there is only a single element left in each sub-list

Step 3: Automatically merge the sub-lists by arranging them in the given order until you get a single sorted list.

Bubble Sort   Bubble sort is also referred to as a comparison algorithm that first compares and then adjusts elements in the specified order. Bubble Sort Algorithm could be explained in the following manner:

Step 1: Beginning from the first element, the algorithm progressively compares elements of an array

Step 2: If the current element and the next element are not in the specified order, interchange the elements

Step 3: If the current element and the next element are in the specified order, you can move on to the next element.

Insertion Sort   Insertion sort algorithm picks one element of a given list at a time and places it at the exact spot where it is to be placed:

Step 1: Compare the first element with the next element and if the element to the left and the key element is not in order, swap them

Step 2: Take the next element and if the new key element should be repositioned, shift the elements of the list towards the right until an appropriate place is created for the element under consideration

Step 3: Go on with Step 2 until all elements of the given list are sorted.

Selection Sort   The selection sort algorithm is used to divide the given list into two halves where the first half will be the sorted list and the second is an unsorted list. To begin with, the sorted list is empty and all elements to be sorted are present in the unsorted list. The Selection sort algorithm will look at all the elements present in the unsorted list, choose the item that is supposed to come first, and then place it in the sorted list. It then repeats the searching process and places the next element to the right of the first element in the sorted list.

For instance, if you have to sort the elements in ascending order, the selection sort algorithm will take a look at the complete list, select the smallest element, and then places that element as the first element in the sorted list:

Step 1: Pick the first element as the minimum and compare it with the next element. If the next element is less than the selected element, mark that as the minimum and compare it with the next element. Repeat the same process until you compare all the elements of the unsorted list.

Step 2: Locate the minimum in the sorted array.

Step 3: Increment the position of the counter to point at the first element of the unsorted array and repeat Steps 1 and 2 for all the elements of the unsorted array.

Searching Algorithms

Searching algorithms are used to search for or seek particular elements that are stored in some given dataset. There are many types of search algorithms such as Linear Search,

Binary Search, Exponential Search, Interpolation search, etc. In this chapter, we shall cover Linear and Binary Search algorithms.

Linear Search: The linear search algorithm is applied to search for a given element successively by comparing it with other items of the given array. It is one of the simplest, most basic searching algorithms but very important so as to understand other sorting algorithms. Linear search algorithm functions in the following way:

Step 1: Create a function that accepts the data list, the length of the list and its key elements

Step 2: If an element present in the given list matches the key element, return the corresponding index number

Step 3: If the element is not found, return -1.

Binary Search: Binary search is used to search for a specific element in a sorted array by applying the Divide and Conquer Algorithm. Here, the algorithm starts with comparing the first element with the middle item and then dividing the array in half. The left half is searched if the element to be searched for is smaller than the middle element and vice versa. Then appropriate sub-arrays are again divided into half and the process is repeated again:

Step 1: Compare the key with the middle element

Step 2: If matched, return the middle index value

Step 3: If the key element is greater than the middle element, search for the key element towards the right of the middle element, else search to the left of it.

Algorithm Analysis

Algorithms can be observed and analyzed both before and after their implementation. These analyses are referred to as A Priori Analysis and A Posterior Analysis.

A Priori Analysis (also known as Theoretical Analysis): tracks the efficiency of algorithms by presuming that all the other factors are constant and do not affect the implementation of the algorithm.

A Posterior Analysis (also known as Empirical Analysis): analyze the algorithms after it was implemented using some programming language. So in this analysis, the actual values like time complexity or execution time of an algorithm, space complexity, or the space required by the algorithm for its full life cycle are gathered.

BASIC FUNCTIONS

A function is a set of organized, reusable code that is applied to perform a single action. As you already know, Python has many built-in functions like print(), but also lets you create your own functions or so-called user-defined functions. In general, functions not only provide better modularity for your application but also ensure a high degree of code reusing. There are simple rules on how to define a function in Python – function blocks begin with the keyword def followed by the function name and parentheses (()) and any input parameters or arguments you have, must be placed within these parentheses. You can also define parameters inside these parentheses.

The first statement of a function could be an optional statement – the documentation string of the function or docstring. The code block within every function starts with a colon (:) and is indented. The statement return [expression] exits a function, optionally passing back an expression to the caller. A return statement with no arguments is the same as a return None. The following is Python set of built-in functions:[5]

Function	Description
abs()	Returns the absolute value of a number
all()	Returns True if all items in an iterable object are true
any()	Returns True if any item in an iterable object is true
ascii()	Returns a readable version of an object. Replaces none-ascii characters with escape character
bin()	Returns the binary version of a number
bool()	Returns the boolean value of the specified object
bytearray()	Returns an array of bytes
bytes()	Returns a bytes object
callable()	Returns True if the specified object is callable, otherwise False
chr()	Returns a character from the specified Unicode code.
classmethod()	Converts a method into a class method
compile()	Returns the specified source as an object, ready to be executed
complex()	Returns a complex number
delattr()	Deletes the specified attribute (property or method) from the specified object

(Continued)

---

[5] https://www.w3schools.com/python/python_ref_functions.asp, W3Schools

Function	Description
dict()	Returns a dictionary (Array)
dir()	Returns a list of the specified object's properties and methods
divmod()	Returns the quotient and the remainder when argument1 is divided by argument2
enumerate()	Takes a collection (e.g. a tuple) and returns it as an enumerate object
eval()	Evaluates and executes an expression
exec()	Executes the specified code (or object)
filter()	Use a filter function to exclude items in an iterable object
float()	Returns a floating point number
format()	Formats a specified value
frozenset()	Returns a frozenset object
getattr()	Returns the value of the specified attribute (property or method)
globals()	Returns the current global symbol table as a dictionary
hasattr()	Returns True if the specified object has the specified attribute (property/method)
hash()	Returns the hash value of a specified object
help()	Executes the built-in help system
hex()	Converts a number into a hexadecimal value
id()	Returns the id of an object
input()	Allowing user input
int()	Returns an integer number
isinstance()	Returns True if a specified object is an instance of a specified object
issubclass()	Returns True if a specified class is a subclass of a specified object
iter()	Returns an iterator object
len()	Returns the length of an object
list()	Returns a list

(Continued)

Function	Description
locals()	Returns an updated dictionary of the current local symbol table
map()	Returns the specified iterator with the specified function applied to each item
max()	Returns the largest item in an iterable
memoryview()	Returns a memory view object
min()	Returns the smallest item in an iterable
next()	Returns the next item in an iterable
object()	Returns a new object
oct()	Converts a number into an octal
open()	Opens a file and returns a file object
ord()	Convert an integer representing the Unicode of the specified character
pow()	Returns the value of x to the power of y
print()	Prints to the standard output device
property()	Gets, sets, deletes a property
range()	Returns a sequence of numbers, starting from 0 and increments by 1 (by default)
repr()	Returns a readable version of an object
reversed()	Returns a reversed iterator
round()	Rounds a numbers
set()	Returns a new set object
setattr()	Sets an attribute (property/method) of an object
slice()	Returns a slice object
sorted()	Returns a sorted list
@staticmethod()	Converts a method into a static method
str()	Returns a string object
sum()	Sums the items of an iterator
super()	Returns an object that represents the parent class
tuple()	Returns a tuple
type()	Returns the type of an object
vars()	Returns the __dict__ property of an object
zip()	Returns an iterator, from two or more iterators

DYNAMIC PROGRAMMING

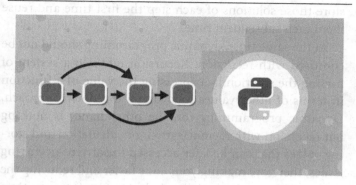

Dynamic programming is a great approach that can be applied to a set of problems for finding an efficient and optimal solution. To put it simply, the idea behind dynamic programming is to divide the problems into sub-problems and store the result for the future so that you do not have to compute that same problem all over again. Such optimization of sub-problems that seeks the overall solution is known as optimal substructure property.

Dynamic programming was designed as a problem-solving technique for resolving complex problems by recursively breaking them up into sub-problems, which then could be each solved one by one. Therefore, dynamic programming uses recursive programming and helps to save the time of re-computing inputs later. However, this approach differs from the Divide and Conquer paradigm in that sub-problems in dynamic programming solutions are intertwined, so some of the same identical steps needed to solve one sub-problem are also saved until needed for other sub-problems. This leads us to the main key point of dynamic programming. Instead of recomputing some of the shared steps, dynamic programming lets us simply store those solutions of each step the first time and reuse them each subsequent time.

At the same time, dynamic programming should not be confused with recursion. Recursion refers to a system of finding the solution by expressing the value of a function in terms of other values following a top-down approach. Dynamic programming, on the other hand, is nothing but recursion with memorization, or calculation and storing values that can be later accessed to solve re-occurring issues, therefore making your code faster and reducing the time complexity. Here, the underlining idea is to save time by efficient use of space. Recursion might take time but no does not need space while dynamic programming requires storage space to stock solutions to sub-problems for potential reference.

And even though the two systems are closely connected, dynamic programming is still favored whenever possible. It mostly happens because brute force recursive programs tend to repeat work when faced with overlapping processes, spending precious time and resources for calculation. Dynamic programming prevents this issue by making sure each identical step is only completed once, storing that step's results in a collector such as a hash table or an array. With that, dynamic programming ensures less repeated work and has a better runtime efficiency.

There are two ways in which dynamic programming can be applied – using top-down or bottom-up approaches.

With the top-down method, the problem is broken down and if some parts of the problem are solved already then the saved value is found and returned, otherwise, the value of the function is memorized or calculated for the first time.

A top-down solution makes sure to reach the base case of every problem by breaking it into smaller sup-problems. By using such a style of recursive chain, top-down dynamic programming only solves sub-problems as they are needed rather than solving them all in order. In this case, memoization plays a great role as a tool to handle computationally expensive programs. Memoization could be defined as a process of saving sub-problem solutions in a top-down approach. And because top-down approaches solve problems as needed, memorization also stores data in a non-sequential way. For this, hashtables are the best collection type, as they store data in an unordered way. In Python, top-down is best completed using the dictionary data structure because it is a perfect suit to store unordered data with key/value pairs.

Bottom-up is another operative way to avoid recursion by decreasing the time complexity that recursion leads to. In this case, the solutions to small problems are calculated in order to build up the solution to the overarching problem. Bottom-up dynamic programming solutions start by focusing on the smallest possible sub-problem, called the base case, and then work step-by-step up to each sub-problem. And as each sub-problem is completed, its solution is saved and used to solve the next smallest sub-problem. As a result, these building solutions are expected to make up an answer to the main problem. Tabulation ensures that this process goes with ease. Tabulation can be defined as the process of storing results of sub-problems from a bottom-up approach in an orderly manner. In tabulation, there is no need to choose which sub-problems need to be solved first but instead go on to solving every sub-problem between the base case and the main problem. And since the process is arranged in sequential order, tabulation can use either lists or arrays, as those collections organize information in a specific order.

One might gain a better understanding of dynamic programming and its types with some examples. We shall examine the concept through a basic calculation of the Fibonacci series. Fibonacci series is a simple sequence of numbers arranged in a way that each number is the sum of the two preceding ones, starting from 0 and 1: $F(n) = F(n-1) + F(n-2)$

Recursive Method

```
def r_fibo(n):
 if n <= 1:
     return n
 else:
     return(r_fibo(n-1) + r_fibo(n-2))⁶
```

With this approach, the program will call itself, over and over again, trying to calculate further values. The calculation of the time complexity of the recursion-based approach is going to be around $O(2^N)$. The space complexity of this approach is $O(N)$ as recursion can go max to N.

For example- $F(4) = F(3) + F(2) = ((F(2) + F(1)) + F(2) = ((F(1) + F(0)) + F(1)) + (F(1) + F(0))$ In this method, values like $F(2)$ will be computed twice and calls for $F(1)$ and $F(0)$

---

⁶ https://towardsdatascience.com/beginners-guide-to-dynamic-programming-8eff07195667, Towardsdatascience

will also be made multiple times. There is going to be great number of repetitions that only prove that this method should be disregarded as ineffective for large values.

Top-Down Method

```
def fibo(n, memo):
 if memo[n] != null:
   return memo[n]
 if n <= 1:
   return n
 else:
  res = fibo(n-1) + fibo(n+1)
  memo[n] = res
  return res
```

With this approach, the computation time is reduced dramatically as the outputs produced after each recursion are saved in a separate list which can be reused later. This method deals with series more efficiently than the previous one.

Bottom Down

```
def fib(n):
 if n<=1:
   return n
 list_ = [0]*(n+1)
 list_[0] = 0
 list_[1] = 1
 for i in range(2, n+1):
  list_[i] = list_[i-1] + list[i-2]
 return list_[n]
```

With this code, there is no need to apply recursion at all. Instead, you can simply create an empty list of length (n+1) and set the base case of F(0) and F(1) at index positions 0 and 1. This list is created to store the corresponding calculated values using a for loop for index values 2 up to n.

And unlike in the first recursive method, the time complexity of this code is linear and takes much less time to compute all the results, as the loop runs from 2 to n, i.e., it runs in O(n). This approach could be regarded as the most efficient way to write a program.

LAMBDA FUNCTIONS

Lambda functions in Python and other programming languages have their roots in lambda calculus and an original model of computation invented by Alonzo Church. Back in the 1930s, Alonzo Church formalized a language based on pure abstraction, now known as lambda calculus. At times, lambda functions could also be referred to as lambda abstractions, directly referring to the abstraction model of Alonzo Church's original design.

In general, functional languages get their origin in mathematical logic and lambda calculus, while imperative programming languages are following the state-based model of computation invented by Alan Turing. Lambda calculus can encode any computation, but contrary to the concept of a Turing machine, it does not keep any state. The two models of computation, lambda calculus and Turing machines can be translated into each other. This equivalence is mostly known as the Church-Turing hypothesis.

In addition, functional languages directly derive from the lambda calculus philosophy, adopting a declarative approach of programming that focuses on abstraction, data transformation, and composition. On the other hand, the Turing Machine led to imperative programming found in languages like Fortran, C, or Python. The imperative style involves programming with statements, leading the flow of the program step by step with detailed instructions. This approach has room for mutation and requires a full-on managing state.

The separation in both foundations has some nuances, as some functional languages incorporate imperative features, like OCaml, while functional features have been mimicking the imperative family of languages in particular with the introduction of lambda functions in Java or Python.

Python is not viewed as a functional language, but it adopted some functional concepts from the beginning. Thus, as early as January 1994, map(), filter(), reduce(), and the lambda operator was added to the language.

To make it clear, the following terms may be used interchangeably depending on the programming language type and culture:

- Anonymous functions
- Lambda functions
- Lambda expressions

- Lambda abstractions
- Lambda form
- Function literals

But for the rest of this section, you will only see the term lambda function. In Python, however, we use the lambda keyword to declare an anonymous function, which refers to a function declared with no name. Although syntactically they look different, lambda functions operate in the same way as regular functions that are scripted using the def keyword. The following are the main characteristics of Python lambda functions:

- A lambda function can take any number of arguments but contain only a single expression. Technically, lambda functions are restricted to only a single expression. An expression here stands for a piece of code executed by the lambda function that might or might not return any value.

- Lambda functions can be applied to return function objects.

- Lambda functions are useful when you need a function for a short period of time. This is commonly applied when you want to pass a function as an argument to higher-order functions, meaning functions that take other functions as their arguments.

Other programming languages like JavaScript have adopted a pattern used to immediately execute a Python lambda function. This is known as an Immediately Invoked Function Expression (IIFE). To illustrate with an example:

```
>>> (lambda x, y: x + y)(2, 3)
5
```

The lambda function above is defined and then immediately called with two arguments (2 and 3). It returns the value 5, which is the sum of the arguments.

Python does not encourage using immediately invoked lambda expressions. It simply results from a lambda expression being callable, unlike the body of a normal function. Lambda functions are frequently used with higher-order functions, which take one or more functions as arguments or return one or more functions. A lambda function can be a higher-order function by taking a function (normal or lambda) as an argument like in the following example:

```
>>> high_ord_func = lambda x, func: x +
func(x)
>>> high_ord_func(2, lambda x: x * x)
6
>>> high_ord_func(2, lambda x: x + 3)
7
```

Python exposes higher-order functions as built-in functions or in the standard library. Examples include map(), filter(), functools.reduce(), as well as key functions like sort(), sorted(), min(), and max().

Syntax

As mentioned previously, a lambda form presents syntactic distinctions from a normal function. In particular, a lambda function has the following characteristics:

- It is scripted as a single line of execution.

- It does not support type annotations.

- It can be immediately invoked (IIFE).

- A lambda function cannot contain any statements. In a lambda function, adding statements like return, pass, assert, or raise will only result in a SyntaxError exception.

Unlike the normal function, a Python lambda function is a single expression. Although in the body of a lambda, you are allowed to spread the expression over several lines using parentheses or a multiline string, it still remains as a single expression:

```
>>> (lambda x:
... (x % 4 and 'odd' or 'even'))(3)
'odd'
```

The example above returns the string 'odd' when the lambda argument is odd, and 'even' when the argument is even. It goes across two lines because it is contained in a set of parentheses, but it still stays as a single expression.

Similar to a normal function object defined with def, Python lambda expressions support all the different ways of passing arguments. This includes:

- Named arguments also called keyword arguments
- Positional arguments
- Variable list of arguments
- Variable list of keyword arguments
- Keyword-only arguments

The following examples display options available in order to pass arguments to lambda expressions:[7]

```
>>> (lambda x, y, z: x + y + z)(1, 2, 3)
6
>>> (lambda x, y, z=3: x + y + z)(1, 2)
6
>>> (lambda x, y, z=3: x + y + z)(1, y=2)
6
>>> (lambda *args: sum(args))(1,2,3)
6
>>> (lambda **kwargs: sum(kwargs.values()))
(one=1, two=2, three=3)
6
>>> (lambda x, *, y=0, z=0: x + y + z)(1,
y=2, z=3)
6
```

Decorators

In Python, a decorator is the execution of a pattern that enables adding behavior to a function or a class. It is

---

[7] https://realpython.com/python-lambda/, Real Python

typically expressed with the @decorator syntax prefixing a function. To demonstrate with an example:[8]

```
def some_decorator(f):
  def wraps(*args):
      print(f"Calling function '{f.__
name__}'")
      return f(args)
  return wraps

@some_decorator
def decorated_function(x):
  print(f"With argument '{x}'")
```

In the example above, some_decorator() is a function that builds on a behavior to decorated_function(), so that invoking decorated_function("Python") results in the following output:

```
Calling function 'decorated_function'
With argument 'Python'
```

Moreover, Python lambdas can be tested in a similar way as regular functions. It's possible to use both modules for that – unittest and doctest.

The unittest module operates Python lambda functions similarly to regular functions:[9]

```
import unittest
addtwo = lambda x: x + 2
class LambdaTest(unittest.TestCase):
    def test_add_two(self):
```

---

[8] https://realpython.com/python-lambda/, Real Python
[9] https://realpython.com/python-lambda/, Real Python

```
        self.assertEqual(addtwo(2), 4)

    def test_add_two_point_two(self):
        self.assertEqual(addtwo(2.2), 4.2)

    def test_add_three(self):
        # Should fail
        self.assertEqual(addtwo(3), 6)
if __name__ == '__main__':
    unittest.main(verbosity=2)
```

This test defines three test methods, each of them exercising a test scenario for addtwo() implemented as a lambda function. The execution of the Python file lambda_unittest.py produces the following:

```
$ python lambda_unittest.py
test_add_three (__main__.LambdaTest) …
FAIL
test_add_two (__main__.LambdaTest) … ok
test_add_two_point_two (__main__
.LambdaTest) … ok
```

The doctest module extracts interactive Python code from docstring to execute tests. And even if the syntax of Python lambda functions does not support a typical docstring, it is possible to attach a string to the __doc__ element of a named lambda:[10]

```
addtwo = lambda x: x + 2
addtwo.__doc__ = """Add 2 to a number.
    >>> addtwo(2)
    4
```

---

[10] https://realpython.com/python-lambda/, Real Python

```
>>> addtwo(2.2)
4.2
>>> addtwo(3) # Should fail
6
"""
if __name__ == '__main__':
    import doctest
    doctest.testmod(verbose=True)
```

There are instances when lambdas in Python tend to be the subject of controversies. And some of the arguments against lambdas include:

- Problems with readability

- The exacting of a functional way of thinking

- Excessive syntax with the lambda keyword

Nevertheless, lambda functions are an important part of functional programming that lets you script handy functions without needing to name them. It's a good idea to use lambda functions when you need to secure the shortest way to write or compute something, for instance, when returning a function, sorting by an alternate key, or integrating elements of an iterable sequence with reduce().

Despite the existing debates questioning the existence and functionality of this feature in Python, lambda has properties that provide serious value to the Python language and to developers. When used properly, they are expressive and can make code shorter and user-friendly. It is certain that once you start adding lambda expressions, you will get used to its operability very quickly.

## CHAPTER 5

Python's Executional Model

IN THIS CHAPTER

➤ Learning about Python executional model

➤ Introducing concepts of names and namespaces

➤ Characterizing features of Python Objects and Classes

The foundation of any programming language consists of a grammar/syntax together with an execution model. The execution model is made to specify the behavior of items of the language. By applying it, one can monitor the behavior of a program that was written in terms of that programming language. Consequently, the observed behavior of a running program should match the behavior derived from

DOI: 10.1201/9781003229896-5

179

the execution model. An execution model observes things such as a unit of work, and what are the limitations on the order in which those units of work take place.

Each programming language has an execution model that defines the manner in which the units of work are scheduled for execution. Detailed reports of the execution models specification include those of Python and of the Unified Parallel C (UPC) programming language.

A Python program is constructed from code blocks. A block stands for a piece of Python program text that is executed as a unit. The following are blocks: a module, a function body, and a class definition. Each command that is scripted interactively is a block. A script file that represents a standard input to the interpreter is a code block; a script command that is specified on the interpreter command line with the "-c" option is a code block; and the string argument passed to the built-in functions eval() and exec() is a code block too. These code blocks are implemented in an execution frame. A frame holds some administrative information that is used for debugging and determining where and how execution continues after the code block's implementation is completed. The execution of the Python program has 2 steps: compilation and interpreter.

Compilation is referred to the process when a program is being converted into byte code. Byte code is fixed terms of instructions that represent arithmetic, comparison, and memory operations. The byte code instructions are created in the. pyc file and can run on any operating system and hardware.

The interpretation step involves converting the byte code (.pyc file) into machine code. This step is essential as the computer can only read from the machine or binary code. Python Virtual Machine (PVM) has to understand the operating system and processor in the computer and only then convert it into machine code. Afterward, these machine code instructions would be executed by the processor and with results displayed.

Nevertheless, the interpreter inside the PVM translates the program line by line, therefore, consuming a lot of time. To prevent this from happening, a compiler known as Just In Time (JIT) is added to PVM. JIT compiler improves the execution speed of the Python program and is widely used in all Python environments like CPython which is standard Python software.

NAMES AND NAMESPACES

Names in Python refer to objects as well as to name binding operations. The following items could be referred to as names: formal parameters to functions, import statements, class and function definitions, or function names in the defining block. It also binds targets that are identifiers if occurring in an assignment and all names defined in the imported module, except those beginning with an underscore and those used at the module level. A target occurring in a del statement is also considered bound for this purpose. So is each assignment or import statement occurring within a block defined by a class or function definition at the module level.

The variables of the module code block could be viewed as local or global. In case a name is bound in a block, it is a local variable of that block unless declared as nonlocal or global. If a name is bound at the module level, it is a global variable. And if a variable is used in a code block but not defined there, it is regarded as a free variable. Every occurrence of a name in the program text refers to the binding of that name guided by the following name resolution rules.

A scope defines the visibility of a name within a block. In case a local variable is defined in a block, its scope includes that block. If the definition involves a function block, the scope extends to any blocks contained within the defining one, unless a contained block introduces a separate binding for the name. When a name is added to a code block, it is resolved with the nearest enclosing scope. The set of all such scopes visible to a code block is also known as the block's environment. When a name is not found at all, a NameError exception appears. If the current scope is a function scope, and the name refers to a local variable that has not yet been bound to a value at the point where the name is used, an UnboundLocalError exception appears on its turn. UnboundLocalError is counted to be a subclass of NameError.

Consequently, if a name binding operation occurs anywhere within a code block, all applications of the name within the block are utilized as references to the current block. This can lead to errors when a name is used within a block before it is bound. And since Python lacks declarations, it is allowed for name binding operations to occur anywhere within a code block. The local variables of a code block can be defined by scanning the entire text of the block for name binding operations.

In case the global statement occurs within a block, all uses of the name specified in the statement refer to the binding of that name in the top-level namespace. Names are resolved in the top-level namespace by looking out for the global namespace, meaning the namespace of the module that has the information about the code block, built – in namespace as well as the namespace of the module built – in functions. Typically, the global namespace is searched first, and only if the name is not found, the built – in namespace is searched. The global statement ensures all uses of the name.

The global statement locates the same scope as a name binding operation in the same block. If the nearest enclosing scope for a free variable contains a global statement, the free variable is viewed as a global. On the other hand, the nonlocal statement causes corresponding names to refer to previously bound variables in the nearest enclosing function scope. SyntaxError may appear at compile time if the given name does not show in any enclosing function scope.

The namespace for a module is automatically created the first time a module is imported. The main module for a script is always called __main__. Class definition blocks and arguments to exec() and eval() are important in the context of name resolution. A class definition is an applicable statement that may use and define names. These references are organized by the normal rules for name resolution with the exception that unbound local variables are included in the global namespace. The namespace of the class definition becomes the attribute dictionary of the class. The scope of names defined in a class block is limited to that class block, meaning it does not extend to the code blocks of methods – this includes only comprehensions and generator expressions since they are executed using a function scope.

The builtins namespace are typically associated with the execution of a code block and could be found by searching for the name __builtins__ in its global namespace. This should be a dictionary or a module and by default, when in the __main__ module the built-in module is set as __builtins__; and when in any other module, __builtins__ stands out as an alias for the dictionary of the builtins module itself. In addition, __builtins__ can be set to a user-created dictionary to make up for a weaker form of restricted execution. Another thing is that users should not deal with __builtins__ at all because it is considered to be strictly an implementation detail. Users wanting to modify values in the builtins namespace should import the builtins module and optimize its attributes appropriately.

In regards to names interaction with dynamic features, the name resolution of free variables should occur at runtime, not at compile time. There are several instances where Python statements are not allowed when used altogether with nested scopes that contain free variables. When a variable is referenced in an enclosing scope, it is simply prohibited to delete the name, and an error will be reported at compile time.

The eval() and exec() functions cannot be accessed to the full environment for resolving names. Names may be resolved in the local and global namespaces of the caller. The exec() and eval() functions have optional arguments to override the global and local namespace. If only one namespace is specified, it is used for both. In addition, free variables are not resolved in the nearest enclosing namespace, but in the global namespace.

In terms of analyzing the Python executional model, it is also important to pay attention to exceptions. Exceptions are a great system trick of breaking out of the regular flow of control of a code block in order to manage errors or other suspicious conditions. An exception occurs only at the point where the error is detected. It could be handled by the surrounding code block or by any code block that directly or indirectly triggered the code block where the error occurred.

The Python interpreter responds with an exception when it detects a run-time error. A Python program can explicitly call an exception with the raise statement. The final clause of such a statement can be used to specify cleanup code that does not handle the exception but is executed whether an exception occurred or not in the preceding code.

Python also uses the "termination" model of error handling: an exception handler can easily detect what happened and continue execution at an outer level, but it cannot be expected to repair the cause of the error and retry the failing operation. When an exception is not handled at all, the interpreter shuts down the execution of the program or returns to its interactive main loop.

Exceptions are strictly identified by class instances. The except clause is chosen depending on the class of the instance: it must address the class of the instance or a base class instead. The instance can be received by the handler and might carry additional information about the exceptional condition.

SCOPES

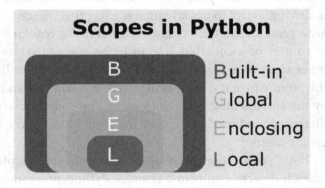

Scopes in Python

B   Built-in
G   Global
E   Enclosing
L   Local

In programming, the scope of a name refers to the area of a program where you can unambiguously locate that name, such as variables, functions, or objects. A name will only be visible to and accessible through the code in its scope. Some programming languages take advantage of scope for preventing name collisions and unwanted behaviors. Most typically, there are two general scopes to distinguish:

global scope (making names that you define in this scope available to all your code) and local scope (making names that you define in this scope visible to the code only within the scope).

Scope was introduced mainly because early programming languages like BASIC only had global names. And with this type of name, any part of the program could modify any variable at any time, so operating and debugging large programs might turn into real misery. In order to work with global names, you would need to monitor all the code in mind and know what the value of a given name is at any time. This was an important side-effect, and some languages like Python decided to implement scope to avoid these issues. When you use a language that implements scope, there is no way for you to locate all the variables in a program, and your ability to access a given name will depend on where you have defined that name. To be clear, the term name here refers to the identifiers of variables, constants, functions, classes, or any other object that can be assigned a name.

The names in your programs can only have the scope of the block of code in which you define them. In case you access the value of a given name from someplace in your code, you will state that the name is in scope. If you cannot locate the name, then you might say that the name is out of scope. Due to the fact that Python is considered to be a dynamically typed language, variables in Python come into existence only when you first assign them a value. On the other hand, functions and classes are available after you define them using def or class. Lastly, modules exist after you import them. As a summary, you can create Python names through one of the following operations:[1]

Operation	Statement
Assignments	x = value
Import operations	import module or from module import name
Function definitions	def my_func(): ...
Argument definitions in the context of functions	def my_func(arg1, arg2,... argN): ...
Class definitions	class MyClass: ...

All the operations above create or, in the case of assignments, optimize new Python names because all of them assign a name to a variable, constant, function, class, instance, or module. However, there is an important distinction between assignment operations and reference or access operations. Thus, if you reference a name, you are just trying to retrieve its content or value. But when you assign a name, you are either creating that name or updating it.

Python utilizes the location of the name assignment or definition to associate it with a specific scope. To put it simply, where you assign or define a name in your code will determine the scope or visibility of that name. For instance, if you assign a value to a name inside a function, then that name will have a local Python scope. In reverse, if you choose to assign a value to a name outside of all functions at the top level of a module, then that name will have a global Python scope.

---

[1] https://realpython.com/python-scope-legb-rule/, Real Python

In Python, the concept of scope is closely connected to the concept of the namespace. As previously mentioned, a Python scope determines where in your program a name is visible. Python scopes are executed as dictionaries that map names to objects. These dictionaries are addressed as namespaces. These are the general mechanisms that Python uses to store names. They are saved in a special attribute called .__dict__.

Using the LEGB Rule

Python resolves names using the widely known LEGB rule, which is named after the Python scope for names. The letters in LEGB stand for Local, Enclosing, Global, and Built-in. In brief, each of these terms means the following:

- Local scope is the code block or body of any Python function or lambda expression. This particular scope includes the names that you define inside the function. These names may only be visible from the code of the function. It's created at function call, not a function definition, so you can have as many different local scopes as function calls. This is true even if you call the same function multiple times, each call is still going to result in a new local scope being created.

- Enclosing scope is a specific scope that is only available for nested functions. If the local scope is an inner or nested function, then the enclosing scope is the scope of the outer or enclosing function. This scope has the names that you add in the enclosing function. And those names in the enclosing scope are visible from the code of the inner and enclosing functions.

- Global scope is regarded as the most important scope in a Python program, script, or module. This Python scope contains all of the names that you define at the top level of a program or a module. Names in this Python scope could be visible from everywhere in your code.

- The built-in scope is a type of Python scope that is created or activated whenever you run a script or open an interactive session. This scope contains names such as keywords, functions, exceptions, and other items that are already built into Python. Names in this Python scope are also available from everywhere in your code. You can automatically load it by Python when you run a program or script.

The LEGB rule is a useful lookup procedure that determines the order in which Python looks up names. For example, if you refer to a given name, then Python will look that name up sequentially in the local, enclosing, global, and built-in scope. If the name exists, then you will be able to get the first occurrence of it. Otherwise, you are just going to get an error.

To summarize, when you use nested functions, names are operated by first checking the local scope or the innermost function's local scope. After that, Python looks at all enclosing scopes of outer functions from the innermost scope to the outermost scope. In case no match is found, Python starts looking through the global and built-in scopes. If no name is found, then you get an error. Regardless, at any given time during execution, you will have at most four active Python scopes – local, enclosing, global, and built-in – depending on where you are in the code. On the other hand, you can always access at least two active scopes, which are the global and built-in scopes that are always available for you.

Functions: The Local Scope

The local scope or function scope is a Python scope generated at function calls. Each time you call a function, you are also creating a new local scope. At the same time, you can think of each def statement and lambda expression as a blueprint for the next local scopes. These local scopes will be produced whenever you call the function at hand. By standard-setting, parameters and names that you assign inside a function exist only within the function or local scope corresponding with the function call. When the function returns, the local scope is ended, and the names are forgotten.

Nested Functions: The Enclosing Scope

Enclosing or nonlocal scope is designed when you nest functions inside other functions. The enclosing scope was firstly added in Python version 2.2. It can take the form of the local scope of any enclosing function's local scopes. Names that you use when the enclosing Python scope is commonly known as nonlocal names.

Modules: The Global Scope

Right from the moment you access a Python program, you are in the global Python scope. Internally, Python turns your program's main script into a module called __main__ to hold the main program's execution. The namespace of this module would be the main global scope of your program. It is also great to know that in Python, the notions of global scope and global names are tightly connected to module files. To illustrate, if you define a name at the top level of any Python module, then that name is considered global to the module. That is also the reason why this type of scope is called module scope.

Once you start working in a Python interactive session, you might notice that '__main__' is also the name of its main module. To check that for yourself, open an interactive session and type in the following:

```
>>> __name__
'__main__'
```

When you run a Python program or an interactive session like the above, the interpreter executes the code in the module or script that serves as an entry point to your program. This module or script is upgraded with the special name, __main__. Meaning that from this point on, you can state that your main global scope is the scope of __main__.

If you want to inspect the names within your main global scope, you can apply dir(). If you call dir() without arguments, then you will get the list of names that live in your current global scope.

But when you call dir() with no arguments, you get the list of names available in your main global Python scope. In the meantime, if you assign a new name (like var here) at the top level of the module (which is __main__ here), then that name will be added to the list returned by dir().

What needs to be noted is that there is only one global Python scope per program execution. This scope remains in action until the program terminates and all its names are forgotten. Otherwise, the next time you were to run the program, the names would remember their values from the previous run. You can access or reference the value of any global name from any place in your code. This includes functions and classes. To clarify these points:

```
>>> var = 10
>>> def func():
... return var # You can access var from
inside func()
...
>>> func()
10
>>> var # Remains unchanged
10
```

Inside func(), you can easily locate or reference the value of var. This will have no effect on your global name var, but it shows you that var can be freely accessed from within func(). At the same time, you cannot assign global names inside functions unless you declare them as global names applying a global statement. Nevertheless, when you assign a value to a name in Python, most likely one of two things is going to happen: you either create a new name or you update an existing name.

The overall behavior will depend on the Python scope in which you are assigning the name. If you try to assign a value to a global name inside a function, then you will end up creating that name in the function's local scope, overriding the global name. This could also mean that you will not be able to optimize most variables that have been determined outside the function from within the function.

Global names, on the other hand, could be updated or modified from any location in your global Python scope. Moreover, the global statement can also be applied to modify global names from almost any place in your code.

Modifying global names is not usually considered to be a good programming practice because it can result in a code that is:

- **Hard to read:** You would need to be aware and understand all of the previous statements that were accessed and used to modify global names.

- **Impossible to reuse:** The code is linked to global names that are specific to a particular program.

- **Difficult to debug:** Most of the statements in the program can change the value of a global name.

Good programming practice typically uses local names rather than global names. Some of the tips include:

- Minimize global name modifications throughout your programs.

- Write self-contained functions that depend on local names rather than global ones.

- Attempt to apply unique object names, no matter what scope you are in.

- Prevent cross-module name modifications from occurring.

- Utilize global names as constants that cannot be optimized during your program's execution.

Built-In Scope

The built-in scope is one of the Python scopes that is managed as a standard library module named builtins in Python version 3. All of Python's built-in objects are located in this module. They are automatically uploaded to the built-in scope once you run the Python interpreter. Python looks for builtins in its LEGB lookup, so you get all the names it defines for free. This also means that you may use them without having to import any module.

You can also notice that the names in builtins are usually loaded into your global Python scope with the special name __builtins__, as observed from the following code:

```
>>> dir()
['__annotations__', '__builtins__',…,
'__package__', '__spec__']
>>> dir(__builtins__)
['ArithmeticError', 'AssertionError',…,
'tuple', 'type', 'vars', 'zip']
```

In the output of the first call to dir(), you can see that __builtins__ is always present in the global Python scope. If you search for __builtins__ using dir(), then you would be able to get the whole list of Python built-in names. On average, the built-in scope has more than 150 names to your current global Python scope. For instance, in Python 3.8 you can get to know the exact number of names as follows:

```
>>> len(dir(__builtins__))
152
```

With the call to len(), you can get the number of items in the list returned by dir(). This returns 152 names that include exceptions, functions, types, special attributes, and other Python built-in objects. Even if you can access all of these Python built-in objects without importing anything, you can also explicitly import builtins and access the names using the dot notation.

MODIFYING THE BEHAVIOR OF A PYTHON SCOPE

To review, by now you should know how a Python scope works and how they restrict the visibility of variables, functions, classes, and other Python objects to certain items of your code. You now know that you can locate or reference global names from any place in your code, but they could be modified or updated only from within the global Python scope. You should also know that you can access local names only from inside the local Python scope they were designed or inside a nested function, but you will not be able to access them from the global Python scope or other local scopes. In addition, you must have learned that nonlocal names can be accessed from inside nested functions, but they cannot be modified or updated from there.

Even if Python scopes follow these general rules by default, there are still ways to modify this standard behavior. Python has two keywords that let you edit the content of global and nonlocal names. These two keywords are: global and nonlocal.

The Global Statement

It must be clear by now that when you try to assign a value to a global name inside a function, you create a new local name in the function scope. To adjust this behavior, you can use a global statement. With this statement, you can make up a list of names that are going to be treated as global names. The statement includes the global keyword followed by one or more names separated by commas. You can also utilize multiple global statements with a name (or a list of names). All the names that you list in a global statement will be marked in the global or module scope in which you define them.

The Nonlocal Statement

Just like global names, nonlocal names can also be accessed from inner functions, but not assigned or updated. In case you wish to modify them, then you need to use a nonlocal statement. Applying a nonlocal statement will let you define a list of names that are going to be treated as nonlocal.

The nonlocal statement consists of the nonlocal keyword together with one or more names separated by commas. These names will refer to the same names in the enclosing Python's scope. The following example shows how you can use nonlocal to change a variable in the enclosing or nonlocal scope:

```
>>> def func():
... var = 50  # A nonlocal variable
... def nested():
...   nonlocal var  # Declare var as
nonlocal
...   var += 50
...
... nested()
... print(var)
```

```
...
>>> func()
100
```

Using the statement nonlocal var, you telling Python that you need to modify var inside nested(). Then, you implement var using an augmented assignment operation. This change is presented in the nonlocal name var, which now has a value of 100. Unlike global, you are not able to apply nonlocal outside of a nested or enclosed function. To be more direct, you cannot use a nonlocal statement in either the global scope or in a local scope. To illustrate with an example:

```
>>> nonlocal my_var  # Try to use nonlocal
in the global scope
 File "<stdin>", line 1
SyntaxError: nonlocal declaration cannot
be allowed at the module level
>>> def func():
... nonlocal var  # Try to use nonlocal in
a local scope
... print(var)
...
  File "<stdin>", line 2
SyntaxError: no binding for nonlocal 'var'
found
```

At first, you tried to use a nonlocal statement in the global Python scope, but since nonlocal only works inside an inner or nested function, you end up getting a SyntaxError telling you that you cannot apply nonlocal in a module scope. In-depth information on the nonlocal statement operations could be found in PEP 3104 – Access to Names in Outer Scopes.

Unlike with global, you cannot use nonlocal to make up lazy nonlocal names. Names should already exist in the enclosing Python scope if you want to apply them as nonlocal names. This means that you cannot manage nonlocal names by declaring them in a nonlocal statement in a nested function. Take a look at the following code example:

```
>>> def func():
... def nested():
...     nonlocal lazy_var  # Try to create a
nonlocal lazy name
...
  File "<stdin>", line 3
SyntaxError: no binding for nonlocal 'lazy_
var' found
```

Using this example you can see that when you try to define a nonlocal name using nonlocal lazy_var, Python immediately raises a SyntaxError because lazy_var is not executed in the enclosing scope of nested().

Using Enclosing Scopes as Closures

Closures are of a specific use case for enclosing Python scope. When you handle a nested function as data, the statements that create that function are placed together with the environment in which they are implemented. The resulting item is known as a closure. To be precise, a closure is an inner or nested function that contains data about its enclosing scope, even if this scope has completed its execution. In addition, closures also provide a way to keep state information between function calls. This can be particularly useful if you need to write code based on the concept of lazy or delayed evaluation.

Some also name this kind of function a factory, a factory function, or a closure factory to specify that the function builds and returns closures, instead of classes or instances.

Bringing Names to Scope with Import

When it comes to writing a Python program, it usually starts by organizing the code into several modules. In order to manage your program, you would need to bring the names in those separate modules to your __main__ module. To do that, you should import the modules or the names explicitly. This is the quickest way you can use those names in your main global Python scope. The following code is an example of what happens when you import some standard modules and names:

```
>>> dir()
['__annotations__', '__builtins__',…,
'__spec__']
>>> import sys
>>> dir()
['__annotations__', '__builtins__',…,
'__spec__', 'sys']
>>> import os
>>> dir()
['__annotations__', '__builtins__',…,
'__spec__', 'os', 'sys']
>>> from functools import partial
>>> dir()
['__annotations__', '__builtins__',…,
'__spec__', 'os', 'partial', 'sys']
```

You start by importing sys and os from the Python standard library. By calling dir() with no arguments, you can observe that these modules are now available for you as names in your current global scope. This way, you can add dot notation to get access to the names that are defined in sys and os. In the next import operation, you use the form from <module> import <name>. With that, you can use the imported name directly in your code. To put it simply, there is no need to explicitly use the dot notation.

Reviewing Unusual Python Scopes

Not all Python structures seem to fit into the LEGB rule for Python scopes. These structures include the following:

- Comprehensions
- Exception blocks
- Classes and instances

Knowing how Python scope works on these three structures will enable you to avoid random errors related to the use of names in these types of Python structures.

Comprehension Variables Scope

A comprehension structure is a compact way to operate with all or part of the items in a collection or sequence. You can apply comprehensions to make lists, dictionaries, and sets. Comprehensions consist of a couple of brackets ([]) or curly braces ({}) containing an expression, followed by one or more for clauses and then zero or one if clause per for clause. Nevertheless, the for a clause in a comprehension runs in a similar way with a traditional for loop. The loop variable in comprehension is local to the structure. To demonstrate with the following code:

```
>>> [item for item in range(5)]
[0, 1, 2, 3, 4]
>>> item # Try to access the comprehension
variable
Traceback (most recent call last):
  File "<stdin>", line 1, in <module>
    item
NameError: name 'item' is not defined
```

If you run the list comprehension, the variable item is deleted and you cannot access its value anymore. It is unlikely that you would need to use the variable outside of this comprehension, but anyway, Python makes sure that its value is no longer accessible once the comprehension is completed.

Exception Variables Scope

Another atypical case of Python scope that you'll encounter is the case of the exception variable. The exception variable is a variable that holds a reference to the exception raised by a try statement. In Python 3.x, such variables are local to the except block and are forgotten when the block ends.

Class and Instance Attributes Scope

When you define a class, you're creating a new local Python scope. The names assigned at the top level of the class live in this local scope. The names that you assigned inside a class statement do not get mixed with names elsewhere. It is safe to say that these names follow the LEGB rule, where the class block represents the L level.

Unlike functions, the class local scope isn't created at call time, but at execution time. Each class object has its own .__dict__ attribute that holds the class scope or namespace where all the class attributes live. It is also possible to access any class attribute using an instance of the class as follows:

```
>>> obj = A()
>>> obj.attr
100
```

If you have the instance, you can access the class attributes using the dot notation, as you did here with obj.attr. Class attributes are specific to the class object, but you can access them from any instances of the class. It is also worth noting that class attributes are basic to all instances of a class. If you edit a class attribute, then the changes will be visible in all instances of the class.

When you call a class, you are making up a new instance of that class. Instances have their own__dict__ attribute that contains the names in the instance local scope or namespace. These names are commonly named as instance attributes and are local and specific to every instance. This means that if you decide to edit an instance attribute, then the changes will be visible only to that specific instance.

If you want to create, update, or access any instance attribute from inside the class, you need to use self along with the dot notation. Self here represents a special attribute that signifies the current instance. On the other hand, to update or access any instance attribute from outside the class, you need to create an instance and then use the dot notation. Typically, when you are writing object-oriented code in Python and try to access an attribute, your program automatically follows these standard steps:

- It checks the instance local scope or namespace first.

- If the attribute is not found there, then check the class local scope or namespace.

- If the name does not exist in the class namespace either, then you will get an AttributeError.

This is the underlying mechanism by which Python locates and solves names in classes and instances. And even classes define a class local scope or namespace, they still do not produce an enclosing scope for methods.

Using Scope-Related Built-In Functions

There is a variety of built-in functions that are closely connected to the concept of Python scope and namespaces. In previous parts, you have used dir() to get information on the names that exist in a given scope. Apart from dir(), there are a few other built-in functions that can assist you in getting information about a Python scope or namespace. We will briefly cover how to work with:

- globals()
- locals()
- dir()
- vars()

Since all four are built-in functions, they are accessible for free in the built-in scope. This means that you can apply them at any time without having to import anything. Most of these functions are designed to be used in an interactive session to get data on various Python objects. Nevertheless, you can find some interesting use cases for them in your code as well.

- **globals():** In Python, globals() is a built-in function that is used to return a reference to the current global scope or namespace dictionary. This dictionary then stores the names of the current module. This means that if you call globals() in a given module, then you will obtain a dictionary containing all the names that you have determined in that module, before the call to globals().

- **locals():** This is another function related to Python scope and namespaces that is responsible for updating and returning a dictionary that holds a copy of the current state of the local Python scope or namespace. Once you call locals() in a function block, you get all the names assigned in the local or function scope up to the point where you call locals(). To illustrate with an example:

```
>>> def func(arg):
... var = 100
... print(locals())
... another = 100
...
>>> func(200)
{'var': 100, 'arg': 200}
```

If you call locals() inside func(), the resulting dictionary is going to contain the name var mapped to the
value 100 and arg mapped to 200. And since locals()
only grabs the names assigned before you call it,
another is not in the dictionary.

If you call locals() in the global Python scope, then
you'll get the same dictionary that you would get if
you were to call globals():

```
>>> locals()
{'__name__': '__main__',…, '__
builtins__': <module 'builtins'
(built-in)>}
>>> locals() is globals()
True
```

When you call locals() in the global Python scope,
you get a dictionary that's identical to the dictionary
returned by the call to globals().

vars(): vars() is another built-in function that returns
the .__dict__ attribute of a module, class, instance, or
any other object which has a dictionary attribute. It
is worth noting that .__dict__ is a special dictionary
that Python applies to implement namespaces.

dir(): You can apply dir() without arguments to get the
list of names in the current Python scope. If you call
dir() with an argument, then the function efforts to
return a list of valid attributes for that object. You can

also use dir() to check the list of names or attributes of different objects that include functions, modules, variables, and so on.

And even though the official documentation says that dir() is designed for interactive use, you can use the function to set a comprehensive list of attributes of any given object. You can even call dir() from inside a function and in return, get the list of names defined in the function scope.

To conclude, the scope of a variable or name determines its visibility throughout your whole code. In Python, scope is executed as either a Local, Enclosing, Global, or Built-in scope. When you apply a variable or name, Python looks for these scopes sequentially to resolve it. In instances, when the name is not found, you will get an error. It is the basic mechanism that Python activates for name resolution and is known as the LEGB rule.

In order to take full advantage of Python's scope to prevent or minimize issues related to name collision, make sure you use global and local names across your programs to improve code maintainability and prepare a coherent strategy to access, optimize, or update names across all Python code. In addition, we have attempted to provide a few scope-related tools and techniques that Python offers and cover how you can use them to gather data about the names that are located in a given scope or to edit the standard behavior of Python scope.

OBJECTS AND CLASSES

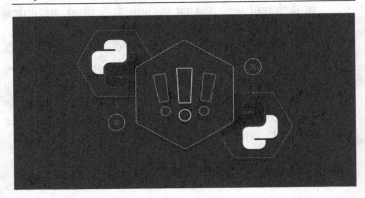

Python is an object-oriented programming language, which means that it comes up with features that allow object-oriented programming. Object-oriented programming became the main programming paradigm used in the creation of new software since the 1980s. It was produced as a solution to maintain the rapidly increasing size and complexity of software operating systems, and to make it easier to change these large and complex systems with time.

Classes in Python are used to provide a system of collecting data and functionality together. Funding a new class creates a new type of object, letting new instances of that type be added. Each class instance can have attributes added to it for carrying on its state. Class instances can also have methods defined by its class for altering its state.

And if you compare Python with other programming languages, Python's class mechanism adds classes with a minimum of new syntax and semantics. It is a great combination of the class mechanisms found in C++ and

Modula-3. Python classes support all the standard features of Object-Oriented Programming: the class inheritance mechanism offers multiple base classes, a derived class can override any methods of its base class or classes, and a method can issue the method of a base class with the same name. Objects can have arbitrary amounts and kinds of information formats. As is true for modules, classes take part in the dynamic nature of Python: they are designed at runtime and can be further edited after creation.

According to C++ terminology, typically class members altogether with the data members are public, and all member functions are virtual. Similar to Modula-3, there are no shorthands when referencing the object's members from its methods: the method function is issued with an explicit first argument representing the object, which is made up implicitly by the call. As in Smalltalk, classes are counted as objects. This provides semantics for importing and renaming. However, unlike C++ and Modula-3, built-in types could be implemented as base classes for extension by the user. As well as that, like in C++, most built-in operators with special syntax could be redefined for class instances.

Normally, the simplest form of class definition looks like this:

```
class ClassName:
  <statement-1>
  .
  .
  .
  <statement-N>
```

Class definitions, just like function definitions (def statements) should be executed before they have any effect, and for that, you can place a class definition in a branch of an if statement, or inside a function. In practice, the statements inside a class definition are usually scripted as function definitions, but other statements are permitted nevertheless. Once a class definition is entered, a new namespace is created, and executed as the local scope – therefore, all assignments to local variables go into this new namespace. But if a class definition is left normally (via the end), a class object is created. This is basically a wrapper around the contents of the namespace created by the class definition. The original local scope is reinstated, and the class object is bound here to the class name given in the class definition header.

Class Objects

By default, class objects support two kinds of operations: attribute references and instantiation.

Attribute references utilize the standard syntax applied for all attribute references in Python: obj.name. Definite attribute names are all the names that were in the class's namespace when the class object was created. Thus, if the class definition looked like this:

```
class MyClass:
  """A simple example class"""
  i = 12345

  def f(self):
    return 'hello world'
```

then MyClass.i and MyClass.f are valid attribute references, able to return an integer and a function object. Class attributes can also be assigned to, so you can change the value of MyClass.i by assignment. __doc__ is also a valid attribute, returning the docstring belonging to the class: "A simple example class."

Class instantiation uses function notation. Just pretend that the class object is a parameterless function that returns a new instance of the class. For instance:

```
x = MyClass()
creates a new instance of the class and
assigns this object to the local variable x.
```

The instantiation operation creates an empty object. Most classes like to create objects with instances customized to a specific initial state. Therefore a class may describe a special method named __init__(), like this:

```
def __init__(self):
  self.data = []
```

If a class defines an __init__() method, class instantiation automatically invokes __init__() for the newly-created class instance. So, in this example, a new, initialized instance can be achieved by:

```
x = MyClass()
```

At the same time, the __init__() method may have arguments for greater flexibility. In that case, arguments given to the class instantiation operator are passed on to __init__().

Objects are individual, but at the same time, multiple names (in multiple scopes) can be bound to the same object. This is known as aliasing in other languages. This is usually not positively recognized at the first glance at Python, and can possibly be ignored when dealing with immutable basic types (numbers, strings, tuples). However, aliasing has a potential surprising effect on the semantics of Python code involving mutable objects such as lists, dictionaries, and many other types. This is usually applied to the advantage of the program since aliases are treated like pointers in some manner. For instance, passing an object is cheap since only a pointer is passed by the implementation, and if a function modifies an object passed as an argument, the caller will see the change – this eliminates the need for two different argument passing mechanisms.

Apart from that, there are also instance objects. And, the only operations that instance objects can manage are attribute references. There are two types of valid attribute names: data attributes and methods.

Data attributes have the same features as "instance variables" in Smalltalk, and "data members" in C++. And similar to local variables, data attributes do not need to be declared as they get activated when they are first assigned to. The other type of instance attribute reference is a method. A method is a function that is a part of an object. Additionally, in Python, the term method is not exclusive to class instances: other object types can have methods as well. For example, list objects have methods called append, insert, remove, sort, and so on. Valid method names of an instance object are based on its class. By default, all attributes of a class that are function objects define corresponding methods of its instances.

Method Objects

Normally, a method is called right after it is bound:

```
x.f()
```

In the MyClass standard case, this will return the string "hello world." Nevertheless, it is not necessary to call a method right away: x.f is a method object, and can be stored away and called at a later time. For example:

```
xf = x.f
while True:
  print(xf())
```
will keep printing hello world until the end of time.

At the same time, you may have noticed that x.f() was called without an argument above, even though the function definition for f() specified an argument. It is the special thing about methods that the instance object can pass as the first argument of the function. In our case, the call x.f() is exactly equivalent to MyClass.f(x). In general, calling a method with a list of n arguments is equivalent to calling the corresponding function with an argument list that is created by inserting the method's instance object before the first argument. Understanding how methods function might require actually working to implement them. Practice will be useful for clarifying any questions you might still hold.

Inheritance

For sure, a language feature would not be given the name of a "class" without supporting inheritance. The syntax for a derived class definition should look like this:

```
class DerivedClassName(BaseClassName):
  <statement-1>
```

```
<statement-N>
```

The name BaseClassName must be defined in a scope containing the derived class definition. In place of a base class name, you can also place other arbitrary expressions. This can be helpful, for instance, when the base class is defined in another module:

```
class DerivedClassName(modname.
BaseClassName):
```

Execution of a derived class definition proceeds the same as for a base class. When the class object is constructed, the base class is remembered. This is used for resolving attribute references: if a requested attribute is not found in the class, the search proceeds to look in the base class. This rule is applied recursively if the base class itself is derived from some other class.

There is not anything particularly difficult in derived classes: DerivedClassName() creates a new instance of the class. Method references are resolved in the following manner: the corresponding class attribute is searched, descending down the chain of base classes if needed, and the method reference is valid if this yields a function object.

Derived classes may override methods of their base classes. Because methods have no special treatment when calling other methods of the same object, a method of a base class that calls another method defined in the same base class may end up calling a method of a derived class that overrides it. An overriding method in a derived class may in fact want to extend rather than simply replace the base class method of the same name. There is an easy way to call the base class method directly: just call BaseClassName.methodname.

Python also has two built-in functions that work with inheritance:

1. You can apply isinstance() to check an instance's type: isinstance(obj, int) will be True only if obj.__class__ is int or some class derived from int.

2. You can use issubclass() to check class inheritance: issubclass(bool, int) is True since bool is a subclass of int. However, issubclass(float, int) is False since float is not a subclass of int.

Python supports a form of multiple inheritance as well. Cass definition with multiple base classes typically look like this:

```
class DerivedClassName(Base1, Base2,
Base3):
  <statement-1>
  .
  .
  .
  <statement-N>
```

For most purposes, you need to keep in mind the search for attributes inherited from a parent class as depth-first, left-to-right, not searching twice in the same class, where there is an overlap in the hierarchy. Therefore, if an attribute is not found in DerivedClassName, it is searched for in Base1, then (recursively) in the base classes of Base1, and if it was not found there, it was searched for in Base2, and so on. This approach is known in some other multiple-inheritance languages as call-next-method and is more complex than the super call found in single-inheritance languages.

Dynamic ordering is necessary because all cases of multiple inheritance exhibit one or more relationships. For example, all classes inherit from an object, so any case of multiple inheritance provides more than one path to reach the object. Dynamic ordering helps keep the base classes from being accessed more than once, and the dynamic algorithm linearizes the search order in a way that preserves the left-to-right ordering specified in each class, which calls each parent only once that is monotonic. Combined together, these properties make it possible to design reliable and extensible classes with multiple inheritance.

## CHAPTER 6

Python for Web Development

IN THIS CHAPTER

➢ Reviewing Python advantages for web development

➢ Learning about the main Python frameworks

➢ Characterizing features of different web development frameworks

Python is a practical language that offers clear and concise syntax. It is also a popular choice for beginners and a powerful tool to back some of the world's most popular products and services from companies like NASA, Google, Microsoft, and many others. One area where Python has the most advantage is web development. Python offers many frameworks including bottle.py, Flask, CherryPy,

DOI: 10.1201/9781003229896-6

Pyramid, Django, and web2py that have been used to power some of the world's most popular websites.

Although it may seem hard to define, creating a website can be seen as a way of building and maintaining a front-end (everything that is visible to the user) and a back-end – hidden from the regular user – which involves all the business logic and exchange with a database. Python positions itself in web development as a back-end language, and it is usually mixed with some other front-end language like JavaScript to build a whole website. At the same time, the reason for using Python in web development is the following: it is a flexible, versatile, and highly efficient programming language that has dynamic typing capacity. Python lets developers create scientific applications, complex system applications with graphics, games, command-line items, web applications, and many other demands.

Another assuring reason for using Python is that it can be used and distributed for free. Because it is known as an open-source product that operates with a broad set of libraries, all the coding information needed is available on the Internet, which means that copying, embedding, and distributing Python in your products is unlimited and unrestricted. This makes it extremely useful in the digital systems space once it conceives flexibility in the marketplace and allows companies to interoperate with many industry sectors. There are other factors that simplify the use of Python for web development:

- **Easy to learn:** The simplicity of the programming algorithms allows you to deal with intricate systems and ease communication between developers working on the same project. In fact, a language that is easy to learn means that new developers or developers who do not have any experience in Python can learn the language and join the development team faster.

- **Good readability:** The fact that Python is similar to our everyday language and its emphasis on readability means that its developers are encouraged to write user-friendly code.

- **Complex tasks on the back-end:** Python is an advanced coding language that enables you to complete difficult tasks on the back-end, including AI and Data Science, as well as any other basic task in other programming languages.

- **Wide range of libraries:** There are a lot of Python libraries that you can use to advance the development of your application. These libraries are packages of pre-scripted code available to everyone, so you do not need to reinvent the core. Some of the libraries include Numpy and scitLearn for data analysis and mathematical algorithms.

- **Good frameworks:** Some of the most widely used web development frameworks for Python include Django, Flask, Pyramid, Web2Py, and Turbogears. These frameworks are similar to toolboxes designed to help you speed up the development of a web application. They consist of packages and modules of standardized code to assist you in several application areas (URL routing, accessing the database, HTTP requests, and responses).

- **Good visualizations:** Representing data in a format can be better understood through using different plots and charts. An efficient way to visually present and comprehend data is to utilize Python libraries that make it possible to visualize data and create clear and easy-to-understand reports.

THE BASIC CONCEPTS AROUND WEB PROGRAMMING

It takes little effort to script and maintain asynchronous code using Python because there are no deadlocks or research contention or any other confusing instances. Each unit of such code runs separately, allowing you to handle various issues faster. Compared to other coding languages, such as Java, Python has a less limited programming method. It has multiple paradigms and can support a multitude of programming approaches, including procedural, object-oriented, and functional ones. This makes Python a suitable language for startups since you might need to

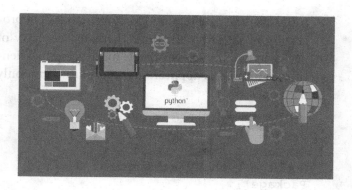

re-assess your approach at any stage. Apart from that, Python has other advantages such as:

- **Fast development:** Python is one of the most rapidly developing coding languages that allow for quick prototyping and iterations. This makes the work easier and far more efficient for developers, giving them a greater competitive advantage.

- **Object-oriented programming (OOP) becomes easier:** OOP is a paradigm that organizes different behaviors and sets of items into several objects and classes. Each of these classes has a function, so if an error occurs in some part of the code, the other parts are not affected. The operation of OOP is considerably simple in Python, which makes development less costly and time-consuming.

- **Rich standard library:** Python's libraries feature a great amount of pre-written code, therefore developers do not need to spare time creating basic items. These libraries also let programmers manage and transform the data required for continuous data processing in machine learning. There are a variety of packages and libraries available for developing scientific and numeric applications. The most commonly used ones are:

```
SciPy (Scientific Numeric Library);
Pandas (Data Analytics Library);
IPython (Command Shell);
Numeric Python (Fundamental Numeric
Package);
Natural Language Toolkit (Library For
Mathematical and Text Analysis).
```

- **Enterprise Application Integration:** Python is a number one choice for enterprise software applications, mostly because of its smooth integration with other languages typically used in enterprise development, such as Java, PHP, and .NET.

Besides, Python calls from and to Java, C++, or C code directly allowing considerable process control and implementation of the most common protocols and data formats. Apart from this, it can be used to combine new and old fragments of infrastructure, which is a typical case in complex mobile applications. Another great thing about Python is that it has various frameworks that simplify the development process. Depending on what you're doing, you may need different frameworks but here are the most well-known Python frameworks:

Django: This framework is well suited for fully fledged web applications and mid-range scalable projects. It has built-in features that allow code re-usage, coherent modification of different code components, and other functionality valued in web development. Django works well with Oracle SQL, PostgreSQL, and MySQL databases.

Pyramid: This framework can be used with various databases and applications or extended with plugins – developers can add any functionality they need. It is particularly useful when you need to implement various solutions in one task.

TurboGears: Framework that has several components such as Repoze, WebOb, and Genshi, and is based on the MVC architecture. It's good for fast and efficient web application development, which is also easy to maintain. With this framework, you can script small or complex applications applying both the minimal and full-stack modes.

Flask: The philosophy behind this framework is to provide a simple solution that can be easily customized. Flask is usually described as a microframework that is commonly applied to small solutions whose main priority is flexible functionality. The framework is also applied for creating prototypes.

Machine learning and artificial intelligence technologies are getting increasingly more attention these days, so more developers are incorporating them into various projects. This is possible if you use well-suited language. Python has efficient packages, options for visualizing results, and goes way beyond data analysis and other characteristics that benefit this area of application:

- **Application Scripting and Software Testing:** Due to Python's strong integration with C, C++, and Java, it can be useful for application scripting as well as customizing large apps and making extensions for them. Python is also used in test automation. Many QA automation specialists choose Python for its simple learning curve, strong community, clear syntax, and user-friendliness.

- **Use in Prototyping:** Creating prototypes in Python is a fast and simple process. The agility of the programming language offers easy code refactoring and quick development of the initial prototype into the final result.

- **Open-Source Perks:** Python has an open-source license that makes it accessible to users and facilitates redistribution and unrestricted modifications. Developers are encouraged to freely use the language and actively contribute to its improvement.

- **Server-Side Scripting:** As mentioned above, Python has a simple syntax, which significantly speeds up the web development process. The code consists of functional modules that allow you to execute the program algorithm based on user actions. Python also supports the graphical user interfaces required in web development.

- **Portability and Interactivity:** Python has a great capacity for dynamic semantics and fast prototyping, which is possible due to its interactivity and porta-bility. It can easily be embedded in a wide range of apps, and effortlessly fix new modules and extend Python's core vocabulary through connecting diverse components.

Nevertheless, despite Python's advantages, it also has a few disadvantages that you should keep in mind if you are considering using this language for your project.

- **Fewer Developers:** When you need to create a web application, you certainly look for the most experienced developers to do the job. However, it is not that easy with Python, since not many expert programmers are working with this language, especially compared to Java.

- **Lack of True Multiprocessor Support:** Multiprocessing is an important part of writing an application. And although Python does support multiprocessing, it might not be as flexible or convenient as other languages. Thus, it can create certain limitations.

- **Speed Limitations:** Python is often criticized for its speed as an interpreted script language, which makes it relatively slower than a lot of its compiled counterparts, such as C/C++ or Java, due to the different methods it applies to translate code.

- **Not the Most Preferred Language for Mobile App Development:** Few companies apply Python for mobile app development, preferring native development for iOS and Android or React Native development.

- **Not Perfect for Memory-Intensive Tasks:** Python is a language mostly known for the flexibility of its data types. This results in fairly high memory consumption and makes it inconvenient to use for memory-intensive solutions.

- **Design Restrictions:** Python is dynamically typed, meaning that it operates some tasks during app runtime that would otherwise be completed in a statically typed language. This puts some limitations on the design. Therefore, if your design is loaded with items, it might slow the program and prevent smooth operation. Because of that, the design you intended might not look as sophisticated as you'd like.

To conclude, Python lets you develop clear and simple applications that are easy to get from a small project to a full-fledged, complex app. Whether you are a new programmer learning how to code or an owner of your startup business, Python could be a suitable option for many types of projects. It is recognized as one of the best programming languages for IT startups – and it is clear why if you compare side-by-side Python's advantages and what startups mostly require. Startups are constantly searching for certainty and reduced risks; they have limited resources, and need room to grow. On the other hand, Python is flexible and easy to modify, does not require too much monitoring, and can be used to build various prototypes.

THE DJANGO FRAMEWORK

As previously mentioned, Django is a high-level Python web framework that enables rapid development and clean, practical design. Django makes it easier to build better web apps quickly and with less code.

Django first started in 2003 by Adrian Holovaty and Simon Willison as an internal project at the Lawrence Journal-World newspaper. It was later released in 2005 and named after the jazz guitarist Django Reinhardt. When the framework was fully developed to handle several high-traffic sites, it became an open-source project with contributors across the world. Django comes with the following design philosophies:[1]

- **Loosely Coupled:** Django wants to make each element of its stack independent of the others.

- **Less Coding:** Less code turns into a quick development.

---

[1] https://docs.djangoproject.com/en/3.2/misc/design-philosophies/, Django

- **Don't Repeat Yourself (DRY):** Everything should be developed only in exactly one place instead of repeating it multiple times.

- **Fast Development:** Django's philosophy is to do everything that is possible to facilitate hyper-fast development.

- **Clean Design:** Django strictly maintains a clean design throughout its own code and makes it easy to follow trendy web-development practices.

Built by experienced developers, Django takes care of much of the web development, so you can focus on writing your application without having to re-adjust any tools. Moreover, the framework is free and open-source; has a thriving and active community, great documentation, and many options for development support. Here are a few more advantages of using Django:

- **Object-Relational Mapping Support:** Django provides an interconnection service between the data model and the database engine and supports a large set of database systems including MySQL, Oracle, and Postgres.

- **Multilingual Support:** Django supports multilingual websites through its built-in internationalization system. With Django, you can develop your website that can support multiple languages.

- **Framework Support:** Django has built-in support for Ajax, RSS, Caching, and various other frameworks.

- **Administration GUI:** Django provides a great and practical user interface for administrative activities.

- **Development Environment:** Django comes with a lightweight webserver to support end-to-end application development and testing.

With the abovementioned characteristics Django can help you write a website or software that is:

- **Complete:** Django strives to provide almost everything developers might want to do "out of the box." Because everything you need is part of the Django service, it all works seamlessly together, follows consistent design patterns, and has extensive and up-to-date documentation.

- **Versatile:** Django can be used to build almost any type of website, from content management systems to social networks and news sites. It can manage any client-side framework and can deliver content in almost any format. At the same time, it provides choices for almost any functionality you might want and can also be extended to use other components if needed.

- **Secure:** Django helps developers avoid many common security mistakes by providing a framework to protect the website automatically. For example, Django provides a secure way to manage user accounts and passwords, avoiding common mistakes like putting session information in cookies where it is vulnerable or directly storing passwords rather than a password hash. Django can check if an entered password is correct by running it through the hash function and comparing the output to the stored hash value. Django enables protection against many vulnerabilities by default, including SQL injection, cross-site scripting, and cross-site request forgery.

- **Scalable:** Django uses a component-based architecture in which every part of the architecture is independent of the others, and can be replaced if needed. Having a clear separation between the different parts means that it can scale for increased traffic by adding hardware at any level: caching servers, database servers, or application servers.

- **Maintainable:** Django code is written applying design principles and patterns that encourage the creation of maintainable and reusable code. To be precise, it makes use of the Don't Repeat Yourself (DRY) principle so there is no unnecessary duplication, reducing the amount of code.

- **Portable:** Django is written in Python, which runs on many platforms and ensures that you are not tied to any particular server and can run your Linux, Windows, and Mac OS X applications. Moreover, Django is well-supported by many web-hosting providers, who often provide specific infrastructure and documentation for hosting Django sites.

Django has continued to improve, from its first milestone release (1.0) in September 2008 through to the recently released version 3.1 (2020). With each release, Django added new functionality and bug fixes, ranging from support for new types of databases, template engines, and caching, to the addition of view functions and classes. Today, Django is a thriving, collaborative open source project, with many users and contributors. While it still has some features that reflect its origin, Django has turned into a versatile framework capable of developing high-profile sites like Instagram, Mozilla, National Geographic, Open, Pinterest, and Open Stack.

Is Django Opinionated?

Web frameworks can often be defined as "opinionated" or "unopinionated." Opinionated frameworks are those with opinions about the "best way" to handle any particular issue. They tend to support rapid development in a particular domain because the best way to do anything is usually well-understood and well-documented. At the same time, they can be less flexible at solving problems outside their main domain and tend to offer fewer options for what components and approaches they can use.

On the other hand, unopinionated frameworks have lesser restrictions on the best way to glue components together to achieve a goal, or even what components should be utilized. They make it easier for developers to use the most appropriate tools to complete a particular task, at the most suited cost.

Following this logic, we could say that Django is "opinionated," and therefore delivers a set of components to handle most web development tasks and preferred ways to use them. However, Django's decoupled architecture means that you can usually choose from a number of different options, or add support for completely new ones if necessary.

What Does Django Code Look Like?

In a typical data-driven website, a web application waits for HTTP requests from the web browser. When a request is received, the application calculates what is needed based on the URL and possibly information in POST data or GET data. Depending on what is required, it may then read or script information from a database or perform other tasks required to complete the request. The application will then return a response to the web browser, often dynamically creating an HTML page for the browser to operate by inserting the retrieved data into placeholders in an HTML template.

Django web applications typically combine the code that handles each of these steps into separate files:

- **URLs:** While it is possible to process requests from every single URL via a single function, it is much more convenient to write a separate view function to handle each resource. A URL mapper is utilized to redirect HTTP requests to the appropriate view based on the request URL. It can also match specific patterns of strings or digits that appear in a URL and pass these to a view function as data.

- **View:** A view is a request handler function, which locates HTTP requests and returns HTTP responses. Views access the data needed to complete requests via models and forward the formatting of the response to templates.

- **Models:** Models are Python objects that give structure to an application's data, and provide mechanisms to manage and store records in the database.

- **Templates:** A template is a text file that structures the layout of a file (such as an HTML page), with place-holders used to represent actual content.

Django refers to this overall file organization as the "Model View Template (MVT)" architecture. It is similar to the more familiar Model View Controller architecture in many ways. A URL mapper is usually stored in a file named urls.py. In the example below, the mapper (urlpatterns) defines a list of mappings between routes and corresponding view functions. When an HTTP request is received that has a URL matching a specified pattern, then the associated view function will be called and passed the request.

```
urlpatterns = [
    path('admin/', admin.site.urls),
    path('book/<int:id>/', views.book_
detail, name='book_detail'),
    path('catalog/', include('catalog.
urls')),
    re_path(r'^([0-9]+)/$', views.best),
]
```

The urlpatterns object is a list of path() and/or re_path() functions (Python lists are added using square brackets, where items are separated by commas and might have an optional trailing comma. For instance: [item1, item2, item3,]).

The first argument to both methods is a route (pattern) that will be matched. The path() method uses angle brackets to define parts of a URL that will be captured and passed through to the view function as named arguments.

The re_path() function applies a flexible pattern matching approach known as a regular expression. The second argument is another function that will be called when the pattern is matched. The notation views.book_detail shows that the function is called book_detail() and can be found in a module called views (i.e. inside a file named views.py)

Handling the Request (views.py)

Views are the core of the web application, receiving HTTP requests from web clients and returning HTTP responses. In the meantime, they maintain the other resources of the framework to access databases and render templates.

The example below shows a minimal view function index(), that our URL mapper could have called in the previous section. Like all view functions, it receives an HttpRequest object as a parameter (request) and returns an HttpResponse object. In this case, we should not do anything with the request, and our response returns a hard-coded string. To illustrate with an example:

```
# filename: views.py (Django view
functions)
from Django.HTTP import HttpResponse
def index(request):
  # Get an HttpRequest - the request
parameter
  # perform operations using information
from the request.
  # Return HttpResponse
  return HttpResponse('Hello from Django!')
```

Defining Data Models (models.py)

Django web applications manage data through Python objects referred to as models. Models are designed to structure stored data, including the field types, size, default values, selection list options, help text for documentation, and label text for forms. The definition of the model is not dependent on the underlying database – you can choose one of several as part of your project requirements. Once you have decided what database you are going to use, there is no need to reach it directly at all – you just write your model structure and Django will complete communicating with the database for you.

The code bit below shows a simple Django model for a Team object. It defines the team name and team level as character fields and specifies a maximum number of characters to be stored for each record. The team_level can be one of several values, so we describe it as a choice field and provide a mapping between choices to be displayed and data to be stored, along with a default value.

```
# filename: models.py
from django.db import models
class Team(models.Model):
  team_name = models.
CharField(max_length=40)
  TEAM_LEVELS = (
    ('U09', 'Under 09s'),
    ('U10', 'Under 10s'),
    ('U11', 'Under 11s'),
    ...  #list other team levels
  )
  team_level = models.CharField(max_length=
  3, choices=TEAM_LEVELS, default='U11')
```

As already mentioned, Python stands for object-oriented programming, a style where you organize codes into objects, which include related data and functions for operating on that data. Objects can also inherit/extend/derive from other objects, sharing common behavior between related objects. It is also possible to create multiple specific instances of the type of object based on the model in the class.

Rendering Data (HTML Templates)

Template systems let you specify the structure of an output document, utilizing placeholders for data that will be filled in when a page is generated. Templates are often applied to form an HTML, but can also create other types of documents. Django supports both its built-in templating system and another popular Python library called Jinja2.

The code below shows what the HTML template called by the render() function might look like. This template has been written under the direction that it will have access to a list variable called very_old_teams when it is rendered. Inside the HTML body, we have an expression that first checks if the very_old_teams variable exists, and then iterates it in a for loop. On each iteration the template displays each team's team_name value in an <li> element:

```
## filename: go/templates/go/index.html
<!DOCTYPE html>
<html lang="en">
<head>
  <meta charset="utf-8">
  <title>Home page</title>
</head>
<body>
  {% if very_old_teams %}
```

```
    <ul>
       {% for team in very_old_teams %}
          <li>{{ team.team_name }}</li>
       {% endfor %}
    </ul>
  {% else %}
    <p>No teams are available.</p>
  {% endif %}
</body>
</html>
```

In the preceding sections, we displayed the main features that you use in almost every web application: URL mapping, views, models, and templates. Just a few other items provided by Django include:

- **Forms:** HTML Forms are designed to collect user data for processing on the server. Django has settings to simplify form creation, validation, and processing.

- **User authentication and permissions:** Django has great user authentication and permission system that has been built to ensure system security.

- **Caching:** Creating content dynamically is much more technically intensive than serving static content. Django provides flexible caching that lets you store all or part of a rendered page so that it does not get re-rendered except when needed.

- **Administration site:** The Django administration site is included by default when you create a website application. It makes it much easier to provide an admin page for site administrators to create, edit, and view any data models on your site.

- **Serializing data:** With Django, it is easy to serialize and serve your data as XML or JSON. This can be particularly helpful when creating a web service that serves data to be consumed by other applications and does not display anything itself, or when creating a website in which the client-side code handles all the rendering of data.

Additionally, Django provides a ready-to-use user interface for administrative activities and automatically generates admin UI based on your project models. The Admin interface depends on the Django.countrib module. To have it working, you need to make sure some modules are imported in the INSTALLED_APPS and MIDDLEWARE_CLASSES tuples of the myproject/settings.py file.

For INSTALLED_APPS make sure you have –

```
INSTALLED_APPS = (
    'django.contrib.admin',
    'django.contrib.auth',
    'django.contrib.contenttypes',
    'django.contrib.sessions',
    'django.contrib.messages',
    'django.contrib.staticfiles',
    'myapp',
)
For MIDDLEWARE_CLASSES –
MIDDLEWARE_CLASSES = (
    'django.contrib.sessions.middleware.
SessionMiddleware',
    'django.middleware.common.
CommonMiddleware',
```

```
  'django.middleware.csrf.
CsrfViewMiddleware',
  'django.contrib.auth.middleware.
AuthenticationMiddleware',
  'django.contrib.messages.middleware.
MessageMiddleware',
  'django.middleware.clickjacking.
XFrameOptionsMiddleware',
)
```

Before launching your server, to access your Admin Interface, you need to initiate the database and create the necessary tables or collections for the admin interface to run. And in order to start the Admin Interface, we need to make sure we have configured a URL for our admin interface. Open the myproject/url.py and you should have something like:

```
from Django.conf.URLs import patterns,
include,
URL
from Django.contrib import admin
admin.autodiscover()

urlpatterns = patterns('',
  # Examples:
  # url(r'^$', 'myproject.views.home',
name = 'home'),
  # url(r'^blog/', include('blog.urls')),
  url(r'^admin/', include(admin.site.urls)),
)
```

Now just run the server: $ python manage.py runserver.

REGULAR EXPRESSIONS

Regular expressions, also called RE, regexes, or regex patterns are tiny, highly specialized programming language codes embedded inside Python and made available via re-modeling. Using this little language, you define the rules for the set of possible strings that you need to match; this set might consist of English sentences, or e-mail addresses, commands or anything else that you like.

Regular expression patterns are compiled into sets of byte-codes which are then executed by a matching engine written in C. For professional expert use, it may be necessary to pay attention to how the engine will implement a given RE, and write the RE in a particular way in order to produce a byte-code that runs faster. The regular expression language is small and limited, so not all possible string processing tasks can be completed using regular expressions. There are some tasks that can be done with regular expressions, but the expressions turn out to be very complicated. In these instances, you may be better off writing Python code to do the processing; even if Python code will be slower than an elaborate regular expression, it will also probably be more understandable.

A regular expression defines a set of strings that matches it. Ultimately, the functions in this module let you see if a particular string matches a given regular expression or if a given regular expression matches a particular string. Additionally, regular expressions can be applied to form new regular expressions; if A and B are both regular expressions, then AB is also a regular expression. By the same logic, if a string p matches A and another string q matches B, the string pq will match AB. Therefore, complex expressions can easily be constructed from simpler primitive expressions.

Regular expressions can consist of both special and ordinary characters. Most ordinary characters, like 'A', 'a', or '0' are the simplest regular expressions; they simply match themselves. Some characters, like '|' or '(', are special. Special characters either stand for classes of ordinary characters or impact how the regular expressions around them are interpreted.

Repetition qualifiers (*, +, ?, {m,n}, etc) cannot be directly nested. This avoids ambiguity with the non-greedy modifier suffix?, and with other modifiers in other implementations. To apply a second repetition to an inner repetition, parentheses may be needed. For instance, the expression (?:a{6})* matches any multiple of six 'a' characters.

The special characters are:[2]

.

In the default mode, dot matches any character except a newline. If the DOTALL flag has been added, this matches any character, including a newline.

^

Caret goes at the start of the string, and in MULTILINE mode also matches immediately after each newline.

$

Matches the end of the string or just before the newline at the end of the string, and in MULTILINE mode also matches before a newline.

---

[2] https://docs.python.org/3/library/re.html, Python

*

Causes the resulting RE to match 0 or more repetitions of the preceding RE, as many repetitions as are possible. ab* will match 'a', 'ab', or 'a' followed by any number of 'b's.

\+

Causes the resulting RE to match 1 or more repetitions of the preceding RE. ab+ will match 'a' followed by any non-zero number of 'b's; it will not match just 'a'.

?

Causes the resulting RE to match 0 or 1 repetitions of the preceding RE. ab? will match either 'a' or 'ab'.

*?, +?, ??

The '*', '+', and '?' qualifiers match as much text as possible. For example, if the RE <.*> is matched against '<a> b <c>', it will match the entire string, and not just '<a>'. Adding ? after the qualifier makes it perform the match in minimal fashion; as few characters as possible will be matched. Using the RE <.*?> will match only '<a>'.

{m}

Specifies that exactly m copies of the previous RE should be matched; fewer matches cause the entire RE not to match. For example, a{6} will match exactly six 'a' characters, but not five.

{m,n}

Causes the resulting RE to match from m to n repetitions of the preceding RE, attempting to match as many repetitions as possible. For example, a{3,5} will match from 3 to 5 "a" characters. Omitting m specifies a lower bound of zero, and omitting n specifies an infinite upper bound. As an example, a{4,}b will match 'aaaab' or a thousand 'a' characters followed by a 'b', but not 'aaab'. The comma may not be omitted, or the modifier would be confused with the previously described form.

{m,n}?

Causes the resulting RE to match from m to n repetitions of the preceding RE, attempting to match as few repetitions as possible. This is the non-greedy version of the previous qualifier. For example, on the 6-character string 'aaaaaa', a{3,5} will match 5 'a' characters, while a{3,5}? will only match 3 characters.

\

Either escapes special characters (permitting you to match characters like '*', '?'), or signals a special sequence; special sequences are discussed below.

It is also worth noting that special characters lose their special meaning inside sets. For example, [(+*)] will match any of the literal characters '(', '+', '*', or ')'. Character classes such as \w or \S (defined below) are also accepted inside a set, although the characters they match depends on whether ASCII or LOCALE mode is in force.

Characters that are not within a range can be matched by complementing the set. If the first character of the set is '^', all the characters that are not in the set will be matched. For instance, [^5] will match any character except '5', and [^^] will match any character except '^'. ^ has no special meaning if it's not the first character in the set.

|

A|B, where A and B can be arbitrary REs, creates a regular expression that will match either A or B. An arbitrary number of REs can be separated by the '|' in this way. As the target string is scanned, REs separated by '|' are tried from left to right. When one pattern completely matches, that branch is accepted. This means that once A matches, B will not be tested further, even if it would produce a longer overall match. In other words, the '|' operator is never greedy. To match a literal '|', use \|, or enclose it inside a character class, as in [|].

(...)

Matches whatever regular expression is inside the parentheses, and indicates the start and end of a group; the contents of a group can be retrieved after a match has been performed, and can be matched later in the string with the \number special sequence, described below. To match the literals '(' or ')', use \(or \), or enclose them inside a character class: [(], [)].

(?...)

This is an extension notation where the first character after the '?' determines what the meaning and further syntax of the construct is. Extensions usually do not create a new group; (?P<name>...) is the only exception to this rule. Following are the currently supported extensions.

(?aiLmsux)

(One or more letters from the set 'a', 'i', 'L', 'm', 's', 'u', 'x'.) The group matches the empty string; the letters set the corresponding flags: re.A (ASCII-only matching), re.I (ignore case), re.L (locale-dependent), re.M (multi-line), re.S (dot matches all), re.U (Unicode matching), and re.X (verbose), for the entire regular expression. (The flags are described in Module Contents.) This is useful if you wish to include the flags as part of the regular expression, instead of passing a flag argument to the re.compile() function. Flags should be used first in the expression string.

(?:...)

A non-capturing version of regular parentheses. Matches whatever regular expression is inside the parentheses, but the substring matched by the group cannot be retrieved after performing a match or referenced later in the pattern.

(?aiLmsux-imsx:...)

(Zero or more letters from the set 'a', 'i', 'L', 'm', 's', 'u', 'x', optionally followed by '-' followed by one or more letters from the 'i', 'm', 's', 'x'.) The letters set or remove the corresponding flags: re.A (ASCII-only matching), re.I (ignore case), re.L (locale-dependent), re.M (multi-line), re.S (dot matches all), re.U (Unicode matching), and re.X (verbose), for the part of the expression. (The flags are described in Module Contents.)

The letters 'a', 'L' and 'u' are mutually exclusive when used as inline flags, so they should not be combined or follow '-'. Instead, when one of them appears in an inline group, it overrides the matching mode in the enclosing group. In Unicode patterns (?a:...) switches to ASCII-only matching, and (?u:...) switches to Unicode matching (default). In byte pattern (?L:...) switches to locale depending matching, and (?a:...) switches to ASCII-only matching (default). This override is only in effect for the narrow inline group, and the original matching mode is restored outside of the group.

(?P<name>...)

Similar to regular parentheses, but the substring matched by the group is accessible with the symbolic group name. Group names must be valid Python identifiers, and each group name must be defined only once within a regular expression. A symbolic group is also a numbered group, just as if the group were not named.

(?P=name)

A backreference to a named group; it matches whatever text was matched by the earlier group named name.

(?#...)

A comment; the contents of the parentheses are simply ignored.

(?=...)

Matches if ... matches next, but does not consume any of the string. This is called a lookahead assertion. For example, Isaac (?=Newton) will match 'Isaac' only if it's followed by 'Newton'.

(?!...)

Matches if ... does not match next. This is a negative lookahead assertion. For example, Isaac (?!Newton) will match 'Isaac' only if it is not followed by 'Newton'.

(?<=...)

Matches if the current position in the string is preceded by a match for ... that ends at the current position. This is called a positive lookbehind assertion. (?<=abc)def will find a match in 'abcdef', since the lookbehind will back up 3 characters and check if the contained pattern matches. The contained pattern must only match strings of some fixed length, meaning that abc or a|b are allowed, but a* and a{3,4} are not. Note that patterns that start with positive lookbehind assertions will not match at the beginning of the string being searched; you will most likely want to use the search() function rather than the match() function:[3]

```
>>>
import re
m = re.search('(?<=abc)def', 'abcdef')
m.group(0)
'def'
```

This example looks for a word following a hyphen:

```
>>>
m = re.search(r'(?<=-)\w+',
'spam-egg')
m.group(0)
'egg'
```

(?<!...)

This is called a negative lookbehind assertion. Similar to positive lookbehind assertions, the contained pattern must only match strings of some fixed length. Patterns that start with negative lookbehind assertions may match at the beginning of the string being searched.

(?(id/name)yes-pattern|no-pattern)

Will try to match with yes-pattern if the group with given name exists, and with no-pattern, if it does not. For example, (<)?(\w+@\w+(?:\.\w+)+)(?(1)>|$) is a

---

[3] https://docs.python.org/3/library/re.html, Python

poor email matching pattern, which will match with 'user@host.com' as well as 'user@host.com,' but not with '<user@host.com' nor 'user@host.com>'.

\number

Matches the contents of the group of the same number. Groups are numbered starting from 1. For example, (.+) \1 matches 'the the' or '55 55', but not 'thethe' (note the space after the group). This special sequence can only be used to match one of the first 99 groups. If the first digit of the number is 0, or the number is 3 octal digits long, it will not be interpreted as a group match, but as the character with octal value number. Inside the '[' and ']' of a character class, all numeric escapes are treated as characters.

\A

Matches only at the start of the string.

\b

Matches the empty string, but only at the beginning or end of a word. A word is defined as a sequence of word characters. Note that formally, \b is defined as the boundary between a\w and a\W character (or vice versa), or between \w and the beginning/end of the string.

Unicode alphanumerics are the ones used in Unicode patterns, but this can be changed by using the ASCII flag. Word boundaries are defined by the current locale if the LOCALE flag is used. Inside a character range, \b represents the backspace character, for compatibility with Python's string literals.

\B

> Matches the empty string, but only when it is not at the beginning or end of a word. This means that r'py\B' matches 'python', 'py3', 'py2', but not 'py', 'py.', or 'py!'. \B is just the opposite of \b, so word characters in Unicode patterns are Unicode alphanumerics or the underscore, although this can be changed by using the ASCII flag. Word boundaries are determined by the current locale if the LOCALE flag is used.

\d

> Matches any Unicode decimal digit (any character in Unicode character category [Nd]). This includes [0–9], and also many other digit characters. If the ASCII flag is used only [0–9] is matched.

\D

> Matches any character which is not a decimal digit. This is the opposite of \d. If the ASCII flag is used, this becomes the equivalent of [^0–9].

\s

> Matches Unicode whitespace characters (which includes [\t\n\r\f\v], and also many other characters, for example, the non-breaking spaces mandated by typography rules in many languages). If the ASCII flag is used, only [\t\n\r\f\v] is matched. In case of 8-bit (bytes) patterns it matches characters considered whitespace in the ASCII character set; this is equivalent to [\t\n\r\f\v].

\S

Matches any character which is not a whitespace character. This is the opposite of \s. If the ASCII flag is used this becomes the equivalent of [^ \t\n\r\f\v].

\w

Matches Unicode word characters and includes most characters that can be part of a word in any language, as well as numbers and the underscore. If the ASCII flag is used, only [a-zA-Z0-9_] is matched. In the case of 8-bit (bytes) patterns, matches characters considered alphanumeric in the ASCII character set, equivalent to [a-zA-Z0-9_]. If the LOCALE flag is used, matches characters considered alphanumeric in the current locale and the underscore.

\W

Matches any character which is not a word character. This is the opposite of \w. If the ASCII flag is used, this becomes the equivalent of [^a-zA-Z0-9_]. If the LOCALE flag is used, matches characters that are neither alphanumeric in the current locale nor the underscore.

\Z

Matches only at the end of the string. The module defines several functions, constants, and an exception. Some of the functions are simplified versions of the full-featured methods for compiled regular expressions.

re.compile(pattern, flags=0)

Compile a regular expression pattern into a regular expression object, which can be used for matching using its match(), search(), and other methods, described below.

The module-level regular expressions define functions, constants, and an exception. Some of the RE are simplified versions of the full-featured methods for compiled regular expressions:[4]

re.A

Make \w, \W, \b, \B, \d, \D, \s, and \S perform ASCII-only matching instead of full Unicode matching. This is only meaningful for Unicode patterns and is ignored for byte patterns.

re.DEBUG

Display debug information about compiled expression. No corresponding inline flag.

re.I

Perform case-insensitive matching; expressions like [A-Z] will also match lowercase letters. Full Unicode matching (such as Ü matching ü) also works unless there.ASCII flag is used to disable non-ASCII matches. The current locale does not change the effect of this flag unless there.LOCALE flag is also used.

Note that when the Unicode patterns [a-z] or [A-Z] are used in combination with the IGNORECASE flag,

---

[4] https://docs.python.org/3/library/re.html, Python

they will match the 52 ASCII letters and 4 additional non-ASCII letters: 'İ' (U+0130, Latin capital letter I with dot above), 'ı' (U+0131, Latin small letter dotless i), 'ſ' (U+017F, Latin small letter longs), and 'K' (U+212A, Kelvin sign). If the ASCII flag is used, only letters 'a' to 'z' and 'A' to 'Z' are matched.

re.L

Make \w, \W, \b, \B, and case-insensitive matching dependent on the current locale. This flag can be applied only with bytes patterns. The use of this flag is discouraged as the locale mechanism is very unreliable, it only handles one "culture" at a time, and it only works with 8-bit locales. Unicode matching is already enabled by default in Python 3 for Unicode (str) patterns, and it is able to handle different locales/languages. Corresponds to the inline flag (?L).

re.M

When specified, the pattern character '^' matches at the beginning of the string and at the beginning of each line (immediately following each newline); and the pattern character '$' matches at the end of the string and at the end of each line (immediately preceding each newline). By default, '^' matches only at the beginning of the string, and '$' only at the end of the string and immediately before the newline (if any) at the end of the string. Corresponds to the inline flag (?m).

re.S

Make the '.' special character match any character at all, including a newline; without this flag, '.' will match anything except a newline. Corresponds to the inline flag (?s).

re.X

This flag allows you to write regular expressions that look simpler and are more readable by allowing you to visually separate logical sections of the pattern and add comments. Whitespace within the pattern is ignored, except when in a character class, or when preceded by an unescaped backslash, or within tokens like *?, (?: or (?P<…>. When a line contains a # that is not in a character class and is not preceded by an unescaped backslash, all characters from the leftmost such # through the end of the line are ignored. This means that the two following regular expression objects that match a decimal number are functionally equal:

```
a = re.compile(r"""\d +  # the integral
part
        \.    # the decimal point
        \d *  # some fractional
digits""", re.X)
b = re.compile(r"\d+\.\d*")
```

Corresponds to the inline flag (?x).

re.search(pattern, string, flags=0)

Scan through string looking for the first location where the regular expression pattern produces a match, and return a corresponding match object. Return None if no position in the string matches the pattern; note that this is different from finding a zero-length match at some point in the string.

re.match(pattern, string, flags=0)

If zero or more characters at the beginning of string match the regular expression pattern, return a corresponding match object. Return None if the string does not match the pattern; note that this is different from a zero-length match.

Note that even in MULTILINE mode, re.match() will only match at the beginning of the string and not at the beginning of each line.

If you want to locate a match anywhere in string, use search() instead (see also search() vs. match()).

re.fullmatch(pattern, string, flags=0)

If the whole string matches the regular expression pattern, return a corresponding match object. Return None, if the string does not match the pattern; note that this is different from a zero-length match.

re.split(pattern, string, maxsplit=0, flags=0)

Split string by the occurrences of pattern. If capturing parentheses are used in the pattern, then the text of all groups in the pattern is also returned as part of the resulting list. If max split is nonzero, at most max split splits occur, and the remainder of the string is returned as the final element of the list.

re.findall(pattern, string, flags=0)

Return all non-overlapping matches of pattern in a string as a list of strings. The string is scanned left-to-right, and matches are returned in the order found. If one or more groups are present in the pattern, return a list of groups; this will be a list of tuples if the pattern has more than one group. Empty matches are included in the result and non-empty matches can start just after a previous empty match.

re.finditer(pattern, string, flags=0)

Return an iterator yielding match objects over all non-overlapping matches for the RE pattern in string. The string is scanned left-to-right, and matches are returned in the order found. Empty matches are included in the result and non-empty matches can now start just after a previous empty match.

re.sub(pattern, repl, string, count=0, flags=0)

Return the string obtained by replacing the leftmost non-overlapping occurrences of pattern in string with the replacement repl. If the pattern is not found, string is returned unchanged. repl can be a string or a function; if it is a string, any backslash escapes in it are processed.

Regular Expression Objects

Compiled regular expression objects support the following methods and attributes:[5]

- **Pattern.search(string[, pos[, endpos]])**: Scan through string looking for the first location where this regular expression produces a match, and return a corresponding match object. Return None if no

---

[5] https://docs.python.org/3/library/re.html, Python

position in the string matches the pattern; note that this is different from finding a zero-length match at some point in the string.

- **Pattern.fullmatch(string[, pos[, endpos]])**: If the whole string matches this regular expression, return a corresponding match object. Return None if the string does not match the pattern; note that this is different from a zero-length match.

- **Pattern.split(string, maxsplit=0)**: Identical to the split() function, using the compiled pattern.

- **Pattern.findall(string[, pos[, endpos]])**: Similar to the findall() function, using the compiled pattern, but also accepts optional pos and endpos parameters that limit the search region like for search().

- **Pattern.finditer(string[, pos[, endpos]])**: Similar to the finditer() function, using the compiled pattern, but also accepts optional pos and endpos parameters that limit the search region like for search().

- **Pattern.sub(repl, string, count=0)**: Identical to the sub() function, using the compiled pattern.

- **Pattern.subn(repl, string, count=0)**: Identical to the subn() function, using the compiled pattern.

- **Pattern.flags**: The regex matching flags. This is a combination of the flags given to compile(), any (?...) inline flags in the pattern, and implicit flags such as UNICODE if the pattern is a Unicode string.

- **Pattern.groups:** The number of capturing groups in the pattern.

- **Pattern.group index:** A dictionary mapping any symbolic group names defined by (?P<id>) to group numbers. The dictionary is empty if no symbolic groups were used in the pattern.

- **Pattern.pattern:** The pattern string from which the pattern object was compiled.

FLASK AND FALCON FRAMEWORKS

Flask is a micro web framework written in Python. It is classified as a "micro" simply because it does not require any specific tools or libraries. It also does not have a database abstraction layer, form validation, or any other components where pre-existing third-party libraries can form common functions. Nevertheless, Flask has extensions that can add application features as if they were implemented in Flask itself. Same extensions exist for object-relational mappers, form validation, upload handling, various open authentication technologies, and several common framework-related tools.

Flask was created by Armin Ronacher of Pocoo, an international group of Python experts formed in 2004. Flask almost instantly become popular among other Python enthusiasts and counts for the second most used web-development frameworks, only slightly behind Django. Applications that use the Flask framework include widely-known websites like Pinterest and LinkedIn.

The microframework Flask is based on several components:

- **Werkzeug:** is a utility library for the Python programming language that could also be treated as a toolkit for Web Server Gateway Interface (WSGI) applications. Werkzeug can produce software objects for request, response, and utility functions. It can also be used to build a custom software framework on top of it and supports Python later versions.

- **Jinja:** is a template engine for the Python programming language that is mostly used to handle templates in a sandbox.

- **MarkupSafe:** is a string handling library for the Python programming language. It extends the Python string type and marks its contents as "safe," and if combined with regular strings, it automatically escapes the unmarked strings, while avoiding double escaping of already marked strings.

- **dangerous:** is a safe data serialization library for the Python programming language, that is used to store the session of a Flask application in a cookie without allowing users to tamper with the session contents.

Main features of Flask also include:

- Development server and debugger

- Integrated support for unit testing

- RESTful request dispatching

- Uses Jinja templating

- Support for secure cookies

- Unicode-based

- Extensive documentation

- Google App Engine compatibility

- Extensions available to enhance features desired

Falcon adds more functionality to the general Python web frameworks by providing extra performance, reliability, and flexibility anytime you need it. It has many advantages to it including the following:

- **Reliability:** Falcon does not have dependencies outside the standard library, helping minimize your website's attack surface by avoiding transitive bugs and breaking changes.

- **Easy to maintain:** With Falcon, it is easy to tell which inputs lead to which outputs. Unhandled exceptions are rarely happening and potentially disturbing behaviors, such as automatic request body parsing, are disabled by default. Finally, when it comes to the framework itself, the scripting logic paths are simple and understandable. All this makes it easier to reason about the code and to moderate cases in large-scale deployments.

- **Fast:** Falcon responds and completes requests significantly faster than other popular Python frameworks like Django and Flask. For an extra speed boost, Falcon compiles itself with alternative programming languages like Cython, and also works well with PyPy.

- **Flexible:** Falcon lets you decide a lot of decisions and implementation details. This option gives you a lot of freedom to customize and edit your organization. It also helps you understand your apps from the basic level, making it easier to tune, debug, and modify over the long run.

The main features of Falcon include the following:

- Native asyncio support
- No reliance on magic globals for routing and state management
- Stable interfaces with an emphasis on backward-compatibility
- Highly optimized, extensible codebase
- DRY request processing via middleware components and hooks
- Idiomatic HTTP error responses
- Straightforward exception handling
- CPython 3.5+ and PyPy 3.5+ support

Using a popular web framework like Flask or Falcon guarantees that you will be able to save a significant amount of both time and money, as well as maintain security and functionality. However, if you still do not know which framework to opt for you should review these important factors that will be able to help you decide:

1. **Technology Changes:** When creating a proof of concept, you may want to use Flask due to its short learning curve and speed in lightweight development. But when it comes time to further developing your product, we may state that Django is the best option to move your project forward.

2. **Support for WSGI:** Web Server Gateway Interface is a standard that permits different computer systems to interoperate with one another. To be precise, it allows a web framework to interact with a web server. This is a great tool when creating an application that lets a developer easily communicate with another online service. Applications may also be judged as WSGI is equipped to handle many requests at the same time. Flask, Django, and Falcon all support WSGI.

3. **Support for Your Framework:** Django, Flask, and Falcon are all well-known frameworks with substantial documentation, thousands of experts and users, and numerous resources built for them. This being said, when creating your product, a sizable and active community is a precious resource that not only saves you time and money but leads to better results.

4. **Type of App:** Your framework choice largely depends on what kind of app is your company building and what will its core features be like. If you are building an app with a sophisticated frontend, Flask or Django are likely your first options. Falcon, on the other hand, is not made specifically for frontend development. However, if you are building an application programming interface (API), Falcon becomes the best choice as it is lightweight, user-friendly, and specialized for that purpose.

5. **Databases:** There is a good chance that you might need a web application that is reliant on a database. Both Django and Flask have a solid database

integration. Both support database migration – the process of modifying and updating your database to hold more or various data. Django and Flask also integrate with SQLite and MySQL, two very popular systems used to communicate with databases. Falcon in this case may not be the best option for a database-reliant application.

6. **Go Open Source:** Open-source software is free to access and may be modified however you want. Django in particular has a large community and fairly regular release times, so you might need to keep track of versions and managing bugs. Make sure to upgrade versions regularly so that your application remains secure and efficient. Using a free, open-source framework with a clear release schedule can make your development team more productive and cohesive as they are prepared ahead of time for the changes.

7. **Application Structure:** Application structure varies depending on the framework you stick to. In particular, Django has a more fixed application structure. Many developers see this as a disadvantage because it limits creativity and obstructs the ability to choose a structure and implementation. Django uses the MTV (model – template – view) architecture pattern that allows you to separate different parts of your program for the sake of better organization. On the other hand, Flask and Falcon are both microframeworks, therefore they do not use the MTV approach, and the way you structure your application is mostly dependent on you.

8. **Routing:** Routing is an important point to consider if you are dealing with any web application with a URL (uniform resource locator). In Flask, there is a decorator located in a Python file that determines certain actions when a specific URL is activated. Django takes a more centralized approach to routing, making Django a more versatile option. On the other hand, Flask makes it easier to extract URL parameters. This is very important for a complex app that has multiple pages and items that interface and pass data to each other through a URL.

Appraisal

Sophisticated programming has become one of the most popular areas to work or invest in. The majority of popular software and data science libraries used for machine learning have Python interfaces, making it the most popular high-level command interface. Python's web frameworks provide fast and convenient ways to produce everything from simple lines of code to full-functioning, data-driven sites. Python's latest versions have strong support for operations, enabling sites to manage tens of thousands of requests per second. In addition, Python also works as a highly efficient code generator, making it possible to write applications that manipulate their own functions that would be nearly impossible to implement in other languages. This coding is named "glue language," meaning it can make disparate code interoperable again. Thus, if you have applications or program domains that you would like to link with each other, you can use Python for this task. Nowadays, Python is generally utilized for writing system scripts, processing big data, performing mathematical computations, creating web applications, and rapid prototyping.

DOI: 10.1201/9781003229896-7

Any crash course or guidelines for dummies on Python is likely to start with installing or updating Python on your computer. There are multiple methods of installation: you can download official Python distributions from Python.org, install from a package manager, and even install specialized distributions for scientific computing. If you are just starting to learn how to navigate Python on your own, the best option would be to start at Python.org. This platform represents the official distribution and is the safest option for learning to program in Python. Moreover, on the platform you can easily get access to a variety of useful tutorials and all sorts of learning materials:

- How to check which version of Python is installed on our device

- How to install and update Python on Windows, macOS, and Linux

- How to use Python on mobile devices like phones or tablets

- How to use Python on the Web with online interpreters

With this Mastering edition, we attempted to outline and contrast how arrays of data are handled in the Python language itself, and how anyone can improve on this. In general, a data type is used to define the format, set the upper and lower bounds of the data so that a program could apply it appropriately. In Python, there is no need to declare a variable without explicitly mentioning the data type.

Instead, Python determines the type of a literal directly from the syntax at runtime. This feature is also known as dynamic typing. Python has the following data types built-in by default, in these categories:[1]

- Text Type: str
- Numeric Types: int, float, complex
- Sequence Types: list, tuple, range
- Mapping Type: dict
- Set Types: set, frozenset
- Boolean Type: bool
- Binary Types: bytes, bytearray

We have also touched upon a concept called comments. Comments are mostly used as statements that are ignored by the interpreter or compiler at runtime. And although comments do not change the outcome of a program, they still play an important role in programming.

Comments are useful information that the developers provide to make sure the reader can understand the source code. Single line, Inline, and Multiline Comments are applied to explain the code's logic or a specific part. Comments are particularly helpful to someone who is trying to manage your code when you are no longer working on it. Additionally, we have covered Python code documentation as a key and continuous course in the process

---

[1] https://www.w3schools.com/python/gloss_python_built-in_data_types.asp, W3Schools

of software development. As a rule, documentation string defines your source code – what your function, module, or class does. In-code documentation works for all modules, and all functions and classes exported by a module should also have docstrings.

Hopefully, you have also been able to learn about Python-centric algorithms and functions for the data structures course. Algorithms are generally written as a combination of user-friendly language and a few common programming languages. There are no distinct rules to form algorithms but you will need to keep the following points in mind:

- Point out what is the exact problem

- Define where you want to start

- Determine where you need to stop

- Decide on the intermediate steps

- Review your algorithm steps

Algorithms may be perceived as paradigms or strategies for solving problems. There are two most common algorithmic paradigms are brute force and divide & conquer. Brute force algorithms are great methods of solving a problem through exercising computing power and testing all possibilities to find a solution rather than using a more advanced strategy to advance overall tactics efficiency. Divide and conquer is an algorithmic paradigm that enables solving a problem by dividing it into smaller subproblems. Once the subproblems are small enough, they will each be solved separately. And in the end, the algorithm repeatedly combines the solved subsolutions into a solution for the original problem. We also took a closer look at some of the important algorithms such as the Tree Traversal Algorithms, Searching Algorithms, and Sorting Algorithms.

Furthermore, Python has many built-in functions like print(), that provide better modularity for your application but also ensure a high degree of code reusing.

And in order to declare an anonymous function, which refers to a function declared with no name In Python, we use the lambda functions. Although syntactically they look different, lambda functions operate in the same way as regular functions that are scripted using the def keyword. The following are the main characteristics of Python lambda functions:

- A lambda function can take any number of arguments but contain only a single expression.

- Lambda functions can be applied to return function objects.

- Lambda functions are useful when you need a function for a short period of time.

The foundation of Python consists of grammar/syntax together with an execution model. The execution model is made to specify the behavior of items of the language. By applying it, one can monitor the behavior of a program that was written in terms of that programming language. An execution model observes things such as a unit of work and the limitations on the order in which those units of work occur. The scope of a name refers to the area of the execution model where you can unambiguously locate that name, such as variables, functions, or objects. A name will only be visible to and accessible through the code in its scope. There are two general scopes to distinguish: global scope (making names that you define in this scope available to all your code) and local scope (making names that you define in this scope visible to the code only within the scope).

Python positions itself in web development as a back-end language, and it is usually mixed with another front-end language to build a whole website. At the same time, the reason for using Python in web development is the following: it is a flexible, versatile, and highly efficient programming language that has dynamic typing capacity. Python lets developers create scientific applications, complex system applications with graphics, games, command-line items, web applications, and many other demands. Another great reason for using Python is that it can be used and distributed for free. Because it is known as an open-source product that operates with a broad set of libraries, all the coding information needed is available on the Internet, which means that copying, embedding, and distributing Python in your products is unlimited and unrestricted. This makes it useful in the digital systems space once it conceives flexibility in the marketplace and allows companies to interoperate with many industry sectors. There are other factors that simplify the use of Python for web development:

- The simplicity of the programming algorithms allows you to ease communication between developers working on the same project. Moreover, a language that is easy to learn means that new developers or developers who do not have any experience in Python can learn the language and join the development team faster.

- Python is an advanced coding language that enables you to complete difficult tasks on the back-end, including AI and Data Science and any other basic task in other programming languages.

- There are many Python libraries that you can use to advance the development of your application. These libraries are packages of pre-scripted code available to everyone, so you do not need to reinvent the core. These libraries also let programmers manage and transform the data required for continuous data processing in Machine Learning. There are a variety of packages and libraries available for developing scientific and numeric applications. The most commonly used ones are:[2]

  - SciPy (Scientific Numeric Library);

  - Pandas (Data Analytics Library);

  - IPython (Command Shell);

  - Numeric Python (Fundamental Numeric Package);

  - Natural Language Toolkit (Library For Mathematical and Text Analysis).

---

[2] https://djangostars.com/blog/python-web-development/, Djangostars

- Python has web development frameworks that include Django, Flask, Pyramid, Web2Py, and Turbogears. These frameworks consist of packages and modules of standardized code to assist you in several application areas (URL routing, accessing the database, HTTP requests, and responses).

- Python is one of the most rapidly developing coding languages that allow for quick prototyping and iterations. This makes the work easier and far more efficient for developers, giving them a greater competitive advantage.

- Object-oriented programming (OOP) operation is considerably simple in Python, which makes development less costly and time consuming.

- Python is a number one choice for enterprise software applications, mostly because of its smooth integration with other languages typically used in enterprise development, such as Java, PHP, and .NET.

As previously mentioned, Python has various frameworks that simplify the development process. We have covered a few of the most well-known Python frameworks:

- **Django:** This framework is well suited for fully fledged web applications and mid-range scalable projects. It has built-in features that allow code re-usage, coherent modification of different code components, and other functionality valued in web development. Django works well with Oracle SQL, PostgreSQL, and MySQL databases.

- **Flask:** The philosophy behind this framework is to provide a simple solution that can be easily customized. Flask is usually described as a microframework that is commonly applied to small solutions whose main priority is flexible functionality. The framework is also applied for creating prototypes.

- **Falcon:** Adds more functionality to the general Python web frameworks by providing extra performance, reliability, and flexibility anytime you need it. It has many advantages to it including stable interfaces with an emphasis on backward compatibility, highly optimized, extensible codebase, and DRY request processing via middleware components and hooks.

Using a popular Python framework like Flask or Falcon guarantees that you will be able to save a significant amount of both time and money and maintain security and functionality. However, when deciding which framework to opt for you should review these important factors that will be able to help you decide:

1. Technology Changes

2. Support for WSGI

3. Support for Your Framework

4. Type of App

5. Databases

6. Go Open Source

7. Application Structure

8. Routing

Python is used widely enough that practically all code editors have used some form of support when writing Python code for the first time. And if you are looking for some additional tools or special guidelines to administer coding in Python, you can search for those in Additional Resources and Developer's Guide: https://devguide.python.org/#resources. There you can find exceptional materials on exploring CPython's internals, changing CPython's grammar, design of CPython's compiler, design of CPython's garbage collector as well as basic Tool support option. Python.org maintenance also includes dynamic analysis with clang and various tools with configuration files as found in the Misc directory.

Index